ABSOLUTE KI

ABSOLUTE KHUSHWANT

The Low-Down on Life, Death and Most Things In-Between

Khushwant Singh

with

Humra Quraishi

PENGUIN BOOKS

PENGUIN BOOKS
Published by the Penguin Group
Penguin Books India Pvt. Ltd, 11 Community Centre, Panchsheel Park,
New Delhi 110 017, India
Penguin Group (USA) Inc., 375 Hudson Street, New York, New York 10014, USA
Penguin Group (Canada), 90 Eglinton Avenue East, Suite 700, Toronto,
Ontario, M4P 2Y3, Canada (a division of Pearson Penguin Canada Inc.)
Penguin Books Ltd, 80 Strand, London WC2R 0RL, England
Penguin Ireland, 25 St Stephen's Green, Dublin 2, Ireland
(a division of Penguin Books Ltd)
Penguin Group (Australia), 250 Camberwell Road, Camberwell,
Victoria 3124, Australia (a division of Pearson Australia Group Pty Ltd)
Penguin Group (NZ), 67 Apollo Drive, Rosedale, North Shore 0632, New Zealand
(a division of Pearson New Zealand Ltd)
Penguin Group (South Africa) (Pty) Ltd, 24 Sturdee Avenue, Rosebank,
Johannesburg 2196, South Africa

Penguin Books Ltd, Registered Offices: 80 Strand, London WC2R 0RL, England

First published by Penguin Books India 2010

Copyright © Khushwant Singh 2010
Photographs copyright © Rahul Singh and Khushwant Singh

All rights reserved

10 9 8 7 6 5 4 3

ISBN 9780143068716

Typeset in Goudy Old Style by SÜRYA, New Delhi
Printed at Thomson Press India Ltd, New Delhi

This book is sold subject to the condition that it shall not, by way of trade or
otherwise, be lent, resold, hired out, or otherwise circulated without the publisher's
prior written consent in any form of binding or cover other than that in which it is
published and without a similar condition including this condition being imposed on
the subsequent purchaser and without limiting the rights under copyright reserved
above, no part of this publication may be reproduced, stored in or introduced into
a retrieval system, or transmitted in any form or by any means (electronic,
mechanical, photocopying, recording or otherwise), without the prior written
permission of both the copyright owner and the above-mentioned publisher of this
book.

CONTENTS

PREFACE	vii
ON BEING A VERY OLD MAN	1
ON HAPPINESS	7
SOLITUDE: THE SECRET OF LONGEVITY	10
ALL ABOUT SEX	15
MY FIRST LOVE	24
LOVE AND MARRIAGE	27
KAVAL AND I	31
MY REGRETS	38
MY BIGGEST WORRY: INTOLERANCE	42
MY WEAKNESSES AND INSECURITIES	45
ON WORK	47
ON BEING A WRITER	50

CONTENTS

THOSE I RESPECT AND ADMIRE	58
JAWAHARLAL NEHRU	72
INDIRA GANDHI	76
SANJAY AND VARUN GANDHI	81
RAJIV AND RAHUL GANDHI	86
ON HONESTY	91
ON THE BRITISH	95
ON DELHI	99
ON PARTITION	105
ON THE 1984 RIOTS	111
THE SIKHS	116
ON COMMUNALISM	124
ON POLITICS TODAY	134
ON PAKISTAN	137
TERROR AND 26/11	145
ON RELIGION	151
ON URDU	164
DESTINY, LUCK, AND FAITH IN HUMBUG	171
ON DEATH	176
ON MYSELF	183
POSTSCRIPT	187

PREFACE

I first met Khushwant in the early eighties. I was looking for a job and went over to the *Hindustan Times* office. He was very courteous. He made small talk for a while and then said a polite but firm 'No'.

About a decade later, my daughter Sarah, who was taking Kuchipudi lessons from Radha and Raja Reddy, had Naina, Khushwant's granddaughter, in her dance class. Around the same time, I was assigned to do a feature on bedrooms of celebrities for *The Times of India*. I called Khushwant, introduced myself as 'Sarah's mother' because I didn't think he'd remember me from the job interview all those years ago,

viii PREFACE

and asked for an appointment to meet him. When I landed up with the photographer, Khushwant introduced me to his wife and proceeded to give me a thorough tour of his house.

Over the years I wrote for various publications and each time Khushwant saw my byline he would call me to tell me he'd read the piece.

In 1996, I lost my father to Alzheimer's. When Khushwant's wife was detected with the same disease a few years later, it was something I could relate to—it brought us closer.

Khushwant is a very special human being. There really is no one like him. His loyalty, friendship, his kindness and generosity, are unparalleled. He's the most transparent person I've met, and yet I've never seen him being rude or ill-mannered. He is also one of the most hardworking people I know. He is childlike in his simplicity and people often take advantage of this. Being sharp, perceptive and sensitive, this is something he is aware of— he realizes he's being used, but he is unable to

PREFACE

say no when asked for a favour. In spite of the image he likes to portray, Khushwant is, surprisingly, extremely conservative. There's a warm, good feeling in his home—you sense it the moment you step in. I have always felt safe and secure there. Spending time listening and talking to Khushwant is therapeutic, as those who've had the opportunity to know him will agree.

It's been a great honour working with him on this book. It's given me an insight into a man I respect, admire and love dearly.

HUMRA QURAISHI

ON BEING A VERY OLD MAN

I am beginning to think there is some truth in the traditional Hindu belief in the four stages of human life: *brahmacharya* or bachelorhood, *grihastha*, the householder, then retiring to a forest, one's natural habitat in *vanaprastha*, and *sanyaas*, solitude. Guru Nanak described what happens to a person who lives into his nineties. In a hymn in Raga Maajh, he says the first ten years of a man's life are spent in childhood, the next ten growing up. At thirty he blossoms into a handsome youth, at forty he is a man. At fifty he starts feeling weak, at sixty he feels old; at seventy he feels the weakening of his senses, at eighty he is incapable of any work

ABSOLUTE KHUSHWANT

and at ninety he keeps lying down and does not understand the reason for his weakness.

I have been fortunate that at ninety-five I am only just beginning to feel what Guru Nanak has written about. I am not prone to lying down but these days I find I need to rest more often. I am a man of habit and have stuck to the same routine for over half a century. I think it's my writing that's kept me going.

I often ask myself why I write. While it provides me my daal, chawal and Scotch whiskey, I could earn as much, if not more, running a dhaba on a national highway. However, writing also boosts my ego, which selling tandoori chicken and parathas would not. Some people read what I write and send me their opinions. It assures me that what I write has some impact, however small. Since some of what I write also gets published in regional languages, chaiwalas at railway stations, ticket checkers on trains, policemen on patrol and butchers in Khan Market make it a point to tell me that they have read some of the stuff

I churn out. I feel mighty pleased with myself. Do any of them change their views after reading what I have written? I am not sure. I believe I was able to persuade some educated sections of my community not to listen to Bhindranwale or consider demanding a separate state. I've also written against religious bigotry. The fundoos never agreed with me because they dismissed me as an agnostic mischief-maker trying to undermine the basis of Indian culture.

I get inspiration from Gurudev Rabindranath Tagore's 'Ekla Chalo' (Walk Alone) when I feel abandoned. I continue to tread the lonely path.

I'm up at around 4 a.m., work right through the day till the evening, till my sundowner. Now I write two weekly columns plus the occasional book review. And I've started working on a novel. I don't know how long I can keep at it and carry on this way.

ABSOLUTE KHUSHWANT

My eyesight is fading, and though I'm lucky I have no serious problems, I'm finding it harder to read and write these days. I enjoy listening to Western Classical on radio, but my hearing is on its way out. I can't watch much TV unless I sit right next to the television set. I usually watch the 6 o'clock news bulletin on NDTV, or Gurbani, and I watch 'Animal Planet' sometimes but *ab woh bhi dekh kar thhak gaya hoon*—those crocodiles, snakes and cheetahs chasing antelopes and eating them up—it's the same every time. I can't watch *Sach ka Saamna*-type of programmes—I find reality shows a big waste of time. Just as I find throwing parties and going to them are. In fact, lately I've even started avoiding meeting people. I get tired very easily and somewhat impatient. I keep thinking about the novel I have to finish.

My morning begins with a glass of fresh orange juice. That's followed by a mug of Korean ginseng tea. Then another two mugs— one of regular tea with a teaspoonful of sugar and milk, and one mug of plain hot water. I

ON BEING A VERY OLD MAN

take all these fluids in the morning to get my bowels moving.

When I was younger and watched my American friends popping an assortment of coloured pills, I used to find it amusing. I don't find it funny any more, because I have to take around a dozen with my breakfast and dinner.

I have a light breakfast of one toast of wholemeal bread and a mug of tea, my fifth of the morning. The toast is accompanied by a capsule of Becosule, two pills of Trefoli, one for high blood pressure, one Zyloric for uric acid and a capsule of garlic oil. At around 11 am I take a mug of hot water with Marmite. I take garlic pearls with both lunch and dinner. I don't take sleeping pills but do have an ayurvedic after-dinner digestive, Sooktyn. I don't take any tonics but am a firm believer in the powers of vitamin C. I suck vitamin C tablets whenever I feel under the weather.

But yes, my heart is still young . . . *dil badmaash hai . . . bure bure khayaal aate hain . . .*

I fantasize. When I fantasize, I'm very happy. Those are my most precious moments. Earlier, when I fantasized in my younger days, I used to go and act out my fantasies, put them to practice. Now, of course, I can't. But there's no censorship on thoughts. Who do I fantasize about? About all those who come to see me? You can keep guessing. It is easy to be honest in one's old age. But an old man is entitled to his secrets, fantasies, Scotch, good company. At ninety-five, this is worth taking the pills for.

ON HAPPINESS

I've lived a reasonably contented life. I've often thought about what it is that makes people happy—what one has to do in order to achieve happiness.

First and foremost is good health. If you do not enjoy good health, you can never be happy. Any ailment, however trivial, will deduct something from your happiness.

Second, a healthy bank balance. It need not run into crores, but it should be enough to provide for comforts, and there should be something to spare for recreation—eating out, going to the movies, travel and holidays in the hills or by the sea. Shortage of money can be demoralizing. Living on credit or borrowing is demeaning and lowers one in one's own eyes.

Third, your own home. Rented places can never give you the comfort or security of a home that is yours for keeps. If it has garden space, all the better. Plant your own trees and flowers, see them grow and blossom, and cultivate a sense of kinship with them.

Fourth, an understanding companion, be it your spouse or a friend. If you have too many misunderstandings it robs you of your peace of mind. It is better to be divorced than to be quarrelling all the time.

Fifth, stop envying those who have done better than you in life—risen higher, made more money, or earned more fame. Envy can be very corroding; avoid comparing yourself with others.

Sixth, do not allow people to descend on you for gup-shup. By the time you get rid of them, you will feel exhausted and poisoned by their gossip-mongering.

Seventh, cultivate a hobby or two that will fulfil you—gardening, reading, writing, painting,

ON HAPPINESS

playing or listening to music. Going to clubs or parties to get free drinks, or to meet celebrities, is a criminal waste of time. It's important to concentrate on something that keeps you occupied. I have family members and friends who spend their entire day caring for stray dogs, giving them food and medicines. There are others who run mobile clinics, treating sick people and animals free of charge.

Eighth, every morning and evening devote fifteen minutes to introspection. In the mornings ten minutes should be spent in keeping the mind absolutely still, and five minutes listing the things you have to do that day. In the evenings, five minutes should be set aside to keep the mind still and ten to go over the tasks you had intended to do.

Ninth, don't lose your temper. Try not to be short-tempered, or vengeful. Even when a friend has been rude, just move on. To carry on and live reasonably well you don't have to be rich or be socially up there—good health and some financial stability are important, but there has to be that focus.

SOLITUDE: THE SECRET OF LONGEVITY

What I enjoy is solitude. I'm fortunate I can spend a lot of time by myself. It is very beneficial to be alone. The mind gets an enormous amount of rest, and a day's silence gives you more energy. If you keep your mind blank for a while—and this is the sole purpose of meditation—you can enjoy solitude and you'll find it empowering. The fact that I'm alone, and sit in silence for most of the day is like meditation. When in Kasauli, I could be alone for weeks at a stretch, exchanging just a few sentences with the cook and gardener who double as caretakers. There's no television set there, and newspapers and a couple of neighbours are my only contact with the outside world. But I don't miss human company, and I'm happy there. Last summer was the first time I wasn't able to make my annual trip to Kasauli; I couldn't have taken that long journey, so I had to remain at home in Delhi. At times I sat in total silence, at times introspecting and happy in solitude.

Even when my wife passed away—we were married for sixty-two years—I sat like this, alone, all night, going over the past. Then, when people kept dropping in, it became tedious. I found it difficult to cope and went off to Goa. Today, my friends and contemporaries have all gone—all. I feel like a solitary traveller left on the road while others have fallen by the roadside.

I never thought of marrying again—not even when I became a widower. Even though mine wasn't a particularly happy marriage, the thought of marrying someone else didn't cross my mind. I've never wanted to be close to anyone. I've never believed in seeking advice or solace from someone or looking for someone to confide in. I don't like the idea of being emotionally dependent on people. I've always managed on my own, even during the worst crises. I don't sit back feeling depressed. Work is the cure of all ills.

There was a brief phase, when there was an injunction on the publication of my autobiography, when I was upset and angry. And the other time I felt low was when my marriage was going through difficulties and my wife threatened to leave me. I went to the Bangla Sahib Gurdwara and spent hours there trying to gather strength to deal with the crisis. But these were exceptions. Generally, I have never been depressed . . . not even when I was sacked as editor of *The Illustrated Weekly of India*. I didn't go into depression but started writing a novel and it was writing that helped

SOLITUDE: THE SECRET OF LONGEVITY 13

me go on. I'm emotionally strong. Even as a child I was known to speak my mind and have rarely ever lied. I hardly ever get angry or hassled. I think one lives a happier, longer life if one is able to get rid of irritants. No matter how big the setback, if you are able to say this one-liner, it helps: 'It doesn't matter . . . I don't give a damn!'

I have had my share of setbacks—and financial insecurities—in my earlier days. What helped me carry on is work. When I was sacked in that discourteous way I drowned myself in work. I decided to complete *Delhi*, which I'd been working on for some years. And after my wife passed away I immersed myself in more writing. I wrote much more than before. I believe in what the Quran and Hadith stress on: Don't waste time. Every single moment should be used. One cannot sit and brood.

Earlier, whenever I was tense, I used to go and visit the cremation grounds. It has a cleansing effect. But now I can't go anywhere. It's work that keeps me going. My writing has been a constant factor. I'm engrossed wholly in writing, and will be till the very end. There's no retirement for me. In fact, in my third year as editor of *The Hindustan Times*, when my contract was due for renewal, K.K. Birla asked me about my retirement plans—whether I'd like to retire. I told him rather categorically, that I'd retire only at Nigambodh Ghat!

Nathaniel Cotton (1707–88) sums up what I feel:

> If solid happiness we prize,
> Within our breast this jewel lies,
> And they are fools who roam.
> The world has nothing to bestow;
> From our own selves our joys must flow,
> And that dear hut, our home.

ALL ABOUT SEX

As a man gets older, his sexual instincts travel from his groin to his head. What he wanted to do in his younger days but did not because of nervousness, lack of response or opportunity, he does in his mind.

If you ask me what's more important, sex or romance, it's sex. Romance is just a gloss, some sort of sheen that wears off, and it loses its lustre very soon.

I've never really had the time nor the inclination for romance. Romantic interludes take up a lot of time and are a sheer waste of energy, for the end result isn't very much. Sex is definitely more important, though sex with

ABSOLUTE KHUSHWANT

the same person can get boring after a while
. . . you know, routine. *Phir wo baat nahin rahti
hai* . . . A partner once bedded becomes a bore.
Even the best-looking man or woman becomes
boring. When it comes to sex, I don't think
looks matter much.

I have many women friends. And I also keep
in touch with those I've made love to in the
past. I can't stand women who are not
animated. She could be the most beautiful
woman, but if she's not lively, then, as far as
I'm concerned, there's no point. I've been with
many women over the years. I've never worried
about infections or sexually transmitted diseases.
You don't think of all this while making love.
You just go for it. Once it's up it has to go in
there—there's no other way!

I've had affairs that I've used as material for
my writing. They contributed to the love-making
scenes and passages in my stories and novels.
The affairs were very good while they lasted
but then you move on, without any
unpleasantness. You just drift apart. And in

ALL ABOUT SEX

the instances where the women have persisted, I've withdrawn after a point—I've always wanted my space and have never wanted anyone to get too close to me emotionally. I value my space and have guarded it because of my writing. I've never had any close friends or deep emotional relationships. Writing is a solitary task and I'm more comfortable being alone. I get impatient with people and places, so I move on. I've been like this all my life.

I have been with women of almost every nationality and they are the same in bed. Foreigners *don't* make love differently; their attitude towards love-making might be different. And all those notions about the French being great lovers or that English women are frigid— they are all myths. Years ago, before I'd travelled to England, I had heard that Englishwomen were frigid, cold and reserved. Nothing could be more wrong. That sort of stereotyping—it's absolute rubbish. Nationalities, even religious backgrounds, make no difference at all. It's the desire, the intensity, that's important; there has to be that attraction. Of course, there could be problems if one of the partners has an insatiable appetite and the other has little interest in sex! As far as I'm concerned, I've never been in a situation like this, so I've never really had any awkward moments.

And like nationality or religious background, size does not matter either—whether it's the size of the penis or that of the breasts, whether the lips are full . . . None of it matters. There just has to be desire on both sides, and reciprocation of feelings. And there should be no suppression or holding back. For if you withhold your urges it will come out in some other form; there's bound to be some aberration. There's far too much sexual frustration in our country and this probably explains the rapes and molestations we hear about every other day. They happen in other countries too, but in India it seems to be a problem now more than ever before. And it's linked to sexual repression and our hypocrisy— we Indians are very interested in sex, we have the curiosity and the drive and we pretend to be prudish and conservative.

I had my first sexual encounter when I was around nineteen. It was 1934. After having spent the summer vacations in Delhi I had to get back to England, where I was studying. From Delhi I took the Frontier Mail to Bombay and had to spend the night there, before the ship set sail the next morning. I spent that night in Bombay's Victoria Terminus Station. I went out to explore the neighbourhood. While I was walking around, I strolled much beyond, towards Kamathipura, Bombay's red-light area—narrow lanes and by-lanes with women looking out of their homes, beckoning, gesturing, smiling ... One of those women kept calling out to me and somehow I found myself responding. 'Which way?' I asked her. She pointed to a staircase leading up to her room. I went up the dark flight of steps. The room was dingy, lit by a single oil lamp. There was a boy sitting there. The woman came forward to receive me. She was fat, dark, middle-aged and dressed in a salwar kameez. Without a word of welcome, she said in Punjabi, 'It will be ten rupees.' I pulled out a ten-rupee note and handed it to her. She gave the boy a five-rupee note and ordered him to give it to her landlord. Then she bolted the door from inside. The room had no furniture save a charpai covered with a greasy durrie and a dirty pillow. There was a pitcher of water and a lota covering its mouth. She turned around to address me. 'You Sardars are such fine-looking men; why do you grow this fungus around your chins?' she asked running her hand over my beard. I did not reply. She sensed I was a novice and asked me whether it was my first time. Hearing me say yes, she slipped off her salwar, tucked her shirt above her waist, baring her fat bottom. She went to the pitcher, filled the lota and splashed water between her thighs and dried her middle with a dirty rag. Then, laying herself on the charpai she raised her legs, bent at the knees, to her chest. 'Come!' she said, stretching out both her arms. Till then I had never had a good look at a woman between her thighs. I was not sure where to enter her. As I undid my trousers and bent over her, she took my penis in one hand and directed it to its target. As I entered her, I spent myself.

The first time I saw female genitals it was a sight! It wasn't attractive or appealing at all—on the contrary, it was appalling! Appalling! I was in my teens and there was a lunch being hosted on the lawns of the teacher's quarters in my school. When this lady teacher tried sitting on the grass, her sari rode up and exposed her thighs and much more. That fleeting glimpse of the teacher's private parts had revolted me but it was also then that my curiosity about a woman's body was whetted and I would try and peep when women labourers were bathing semi-clad ... It was with that glimpse that I first became aware of desire.

Another time, when I was recovering from yet another bout of typhoid, a nurse hired to look after me went beyond her call of duty—she did more than sponge my body. I was still young, in my teens, but that didn't deter her from holding my penis and even kissing it. I was too young to know what was happening, and also too weak and too ill to respond, react or enjoy it.

And long before that, when I was a young child, a cousin tried exploring my body. She must have been around the same age as I was, yet we'd tried touching each other and somehow it aroused something—a strange curiosity about the female form.

I don't think it's only men who seduce. I find that women are often better at the art of

ALL ABOUT SEX 23

seduction. More than me trying to seduce women, it's women who've tried seducing me all these years. Right from the beginning—the very first time I was attracted to a woman, it was she who took the first move—she held my hand in the cinema hall. Even later, with other women too, it was the women, with the exception of one or two cases, who made a pass first, leading me on. I have rarely taken the lead. When I've been attracted to someone, I've had little confidence in expressing myself. And years later, when I happened to tell them how I'd felt, several of them exclaimed, 'Why the hell didn't you tell me before?' Each time I've had a woman make a pass at me I've felt flattered and have reciprocated. Looking back I wish I'd had the confidence to make the first move.

MY FIRST LOVE

She was a Muslim from Hyderabad who had come to Delhi to study Home Science at Lady Irwin. I must have been around seventeen; I was in college then. Ghayoorunnisa was three years older than me. She was my sister's friend. On one of those occasions when she, my sister and I had gone to the cinema, she slipped her hand in mine. That alone meant a lot to me. I was drawn to her and the burkha she wore only added to my attraction. It made her even more alluring, romantic, even more beautiful. Ghayoor died some years ago. On hearing of her death I went to Hyderabad and visited her grave. When I had last met her in Hyderabad

MY FIRST LOVE 25

she was very lonely. She was not in good health and she'd spoken of death. She had even booked a grave for herself. Most members of her family had died and her daughter Fareesa had gone abroad and settled there.

Ghayoor and I didn't end up together, it just didn't happen. I went off to England to study and Ghayoor had gone back to Hyderabad. She got married and settled there. She married twice, actually. I met her again after thirty years, in Delhi, when she accompanied Fareesa for her admission into Lady Irwin College. I continued to keep in touch with her after that and made it a point to meet her whenever I was in Hyderabad. I was so taken with Ghayoor that it drew me to the entire Muslim community. I do believe that if you fall in love your very perception of the other person's community changes. You begin to feel closer to that community. Before I met Ghayoor I'd had stereotypical notions of Muslims—the sort of notions that most Hindus and Sikhs are brought up with. But all that changed. And my attachment for the Muslim community increased in the years that followed. I met and was friendly with many women after Ghayoor, but with her it was different.

LOVE AND MARRIAGE

Love, as the word is understood in the West, is known to only a tiny minority of the very Westernized living in the half-a-dozen big cities of India—those who prefer to speak English rather than Indian languages, read only English books, watch only Western movies and even dream in English. For the rest, it is something they read about in poems or see on the screen but very rarely experience personally. Arranged marriages are the accepted norm, 'love marriages' a rarity. In arranged marriages, the parties first make each other's acquaintance physically, by exploring each other's bodies, and it is only after some of the lust has been drained out of their systems that they get the chance to discover each other's minds and personalities. It is only after lust loses its urgency and power and there is no clash, that the alliance may, in later years, develop bonds of companionship. But the chances of this happening are bleak. In most cases, the husband and wife suffer each other till the end of their days.

I think it's healthy and human to think about sex, and fantasize. I firmly believe that, no matter how happily married you are, the thought of adultery is at the back of your mind. I also feel that most marriages last because spouses don't have the energy to fight a divorce battle. All men, young and old alike, if they are honest, will admit that sex is always on their minds. Of course, my mind is still very active. Though I'm not doing it any longer, I can still write about it. Nobody has invented a condom for the pen. My pen is still sexy.

LOVE AND MARRIAGE

To most newly married Indian couples, the concept of privacy is as alien as that of love. They rarely get a room to themselves; the bride-wife sleeps with women members of her husband's family; the husband's charpai is placed alongside his father's and brothers'. Occasionally, the mother-in-law, anxious to acquire a grandson, will contrive a meeting between her son and daughter-in-law: the most common technique is to get the girl to take a tumbler of milk to the lad when other male members are elsewhere. That's when the boy grabs the chance for a 'quickie'. Hardly ever does the couple get enough time for a prolonged and satisfying session of intercourse. Most Indian men are not even aware that women also have orgasms; and most Indian women, even though they go from one pregnancy to another, share this ignorance because they have no idea that sex can be pleasurable. This is a sad commentary on the people of the country that produced the most widely read treatise on the art of sex, the *Kama Sutra*, and elevated the act of sex to spiritual sublimity by explicit depictions on the country's temples.

These lines of Asadullah Khan Ghalib say it best:

Ishq par zor nahein
Hai yeh woh aatish Ghalib
Ke lagaae na lagey, aur bujhaaye na baney.

There is no power above love
Nor do we know what it is about
It is like a raging fire, O Ghalib
When you want to light it,
    it refuses to ignite
When you want to put it out,
    it refuses to die.

KAVAL AND I

Many who didn't know me or my family were often under the impression that my wife didn't exist or that she was tucked away in some village like the wives of many of our netas. This was, of course, a grievous error, as my wife was quite a formidable character who ruled our home with as firm a hand as Indira Gandhi ruled India. Unlike many modern girls of today, who bob their hair, wear T-shirts and jeans and speak chi chi Hinglish but when it comes to being married tamely surrender their right to choose husbands to their parents, my wife made her own choice over sixty years ago. It was during my stay in Welwyn Garden in my first year in England that I ran into Kaval (Malik), who had been with me at the Modern School. She had been a good-looking, light-skinned girl, a bit of a tomboy, playing hockey and soccer with the boys. When I left school she was still a gawky girl, a couple of years my junior. I had lost track of her when I moved to Lahore. When I ran into her in England, she had blossomed into a beauty and was much sought after by many boys I knew, some from India's richest families. Meeting the girl now grown into a young woman caused me anguish, as I fell desperately in love with her and also felt that I stood little chance of winning her. Amongst other obstacles was the fact that her father was senior engineer with the Public Works Department, while mine was a builder who had to get contracts from the same. Besides, I was studying law, and lawyers, being a dime a dozen, were poorly rated in the marriage market. My only chance was to bypass the parents and approach the girl directly. It was nearing Christmas vacations and she had

KAVAL AND I

33

nowhere to go. I suggested she come with me to the Quaker hostel in Buckinghamshire. She wrote to her parents to seek their permission. To my utter surprise, they allowed her to go. I began courting her as soon as the train left London. On our way back, I asked her if I could ask my parents to approach hers with a proposal. She nodded her consent. I got married in October 1939. It was a grand affair. My wife's father was then chief engineer of the PWD, the first Indian to rise to the position. My father was acknowledged as the biggest owner of real estate in Delhi. There were over fifteen hundred guests at our wedding reception, including M.A. Jinnah. Champagne flowed like the Jamuna in flood. It was a traditional Sikh wedding, with a brass band leading the procession. I was draped in a veil of jasmine flowers, riding on a white horse sword in hand. The Maliks lived on 1, Tughlak Road, which was barely a furlong down the road from my father's house, 1A Janpath. We went through the ritual of being received by the bride's relatives and I had to bear with a lot of banter and practical jokes. This was followed by a feast. I spent the night in the Malik home. Early next morning under a vast canopy we sat in front of the Granth Sahib, her face demurely covered by a veil; I in a cream-coloured sherwani and churidar with a gilded kirpan in my hand .The Anand Karaj (ceremony of bliss) was a solemn affair with ragis singing wedding hymns. I couldn't resist the temptation of slipping my hand under her dupatta, with which she was covered, and tweaking her toes. We went round the Granth Sahib four times, I in front, she following me, holding one end of the scarf I had in my hands. We took our marriage vows—to remain faithful to each other and look upon others as brothers and sisters. It was the morning of 30 October 1939.

The same evening my father arranged cocktails and a dance party on the spacious lawns in front of his house. Among the guests was M.A. Jinnah, who lived across the road and occasionally dropped in to inspect my father's rose garden. We were allowed to retire at midnight to consummate our marriage. I was later told that one of the drunken guests had run his car over a telegraph peon on his way to deliver congratulatory telegrams. I was not told of this at the time. The wedding night is something every couple looks forward to. On ours I discovered that my bride was a virgin. We had never talked of sex till then, nor had she allowed my hands to go exploring beneath her waist. She pleaded with me to be patient. I gave in. The next evening we left for our honeymoon. Mount Abu had been my choice for no other reason than that the entrance of Welwyn Garden City railway station displayed a large poster depicting the marble temple legend with the words 'Visit India: Dilwara Temples at Mount Abu'. My English friends had asked me whether I had seen the place. I had admitted I had not but would do so as soon as I returned home.

A spacious bungalow of the CPWD overlooking the Nakki Lake had been reserved for us. The night was made for loving. We returned to Delhi still hungering for each other's bodies.

I was married for over sixty years. It wasn't a happy marriage. In fact, things had got so bad—we were both in our fifties—we had even contemplated divorce. But when you have a family you have to make compromises, you have to keep up appearances.

I think right from the start my wife felt I didn't match up to her previous suitors; I didn't come anywhere close. She was very possessive and aggressive, and resented it when I, even very casually, met a woman friend. She would sulk. This, in spite of the fact that my wife had, from the very beginning of the marriage, probably from the very first year, got close to one man in particular. Their relationship carried on for about twenty years and this was something that affected me deeply, snapping something inside me, changing something within me forever. I didn't react to her relationship even though I was unhappy. I didn't want to interfere. I never thought of having any affairs myself; neither did I have any on the rebound. I felt I could no longer respond emotionally and had nothing left to give. Emotionally, I felt totally bankrupt.

MY REGRETS

I regret having started my writing career late. Had I begun earlier, I could have written much more.

My father, though himself a contractor, was keen that I become a lawyer. So much so, that after my second year of college at St Stephen's studying history, economics and philosophy, he sent me to the Lahore Government College. And later, much in accordance with his wishes, I started out at the Lahore High Court. And though I practiced there for seven years, I wasn't successful. It was during those years that I started writing short stories. I wrote 'The Raj', 'Karma', 'The Mark of Vishnu' and several

MY REGRETS

39

others, and sent them to some publications in the US and the UK. They were published, and the reviews they got were very good. That's how I came to take my writing more seriously.

It was in the '50s that I wrote my first novel *Mano Majra*—I later changed this title to *Train to Pakistan*. I got my break in journalism in 1965, when *The New York Times* asked me to write on Indo-Pakistan relations. I remember the title they had given the story was 'Why Hindus and Muslims Speak Hate' and had splashed it on the front page. I took up writing rather late in life, after wasting seven years practising law, and I regret that. In any case, lawyers live off other people's quarrels. That's what lawyers do.

My other regret is that I could have played a bigger role in my battle against the fundoos, religious fundamentalists. My columns have a vast readership, and I should have written more against fundamentalists. My battle is against fundoos from all communities. I have spoken out against the Muslim fundamentalists,

ABSOLUTE KHUSHWANT

against Hindu fundamentalists, and though I have no personal quarrel with Advani I believe he has changed the entire map of this country.

He is the one man who has done more damage to the country than any other. He re-created Islamophobia. The tearing down of the Babri Masjid was the single-most horrendous act and we haven't had peace since then.

When I'd first met Advani, years ago, I'd thought him to be a man of integrity and honesty; I even admired him. I'd found him to be a clear-headed thinker and a powerful orator. We'd kept in touch. He came over to condole when my father died and I visited his home a few times. I was charmed by the congenial atmosphere—the family welcomed anyone who dropped in and I always felt very comfortable. When Advani stood for the Parliament elections after 1984, he sent across BJP candidate Vijay Kumar Malhotra to ask if I would propose party President Advani's name and I did so quite gladly. The Sikhs were determined not to vote for the Congress. The 1984 massacre of

MY REGRETS

Sikhs that followed Mrs Gandhi's assassination was fresh in our minds and I had not recovered from the hurt and anger at the Congress message that they had to 'teach the Sikhs a lesson'.

But the day Advani launched his rath yatra, I was disillusioned. The man was sowing the seeds of hatred between two communities and destroying the spirit of the entire nation. I never expected to see the sort of communal hatred and madness that I'd witnessed during Partition but he's fanned those flames again. I hold him responsible for the destruction of communal harmony in our country today.

MY BIGGEST WORRY:
INTOLERANCE

My only worry today is the rise in right-wing fascist parties in the country.

We allowed fascism to dig its heels in our courtyard. We let them get away with every step they took and never raised a howl of protest. Today they burn books they do not like; they beat up journalists who write against them; they attack cinema houses showing films they do not approve of; they vandalize the paintings of India's leading artist; they pervert texts from history books to make them conform to their ideas; they foul-mouth everyone who disagrees with them. We fail to hit back because

MY BIGGEST WORRY: INTOLERANCE 43

we have never been a united force and do not realize the perils of allowing our country to fall into their hands.

Events such as the demolition of the Babri masjid, the burning of Graham Staines and his children and the barbaric and mindless carnage in Gujarat are events that stink of politics mixed with religion. I have always maintained that religion and politics do not go together; they must be kept apart at all cost. What in Nehru's time were parties of marginal importance, the RSS, the Hindu Mahasabha, the Jan Sangh, the Shiv Sena and the Bajrang Dal, gathered strength and became the main opposition to secular forces. The young, the present generation, should be aware of the rise in communal politics and the dangers involved. If India is to survive as a nation and march forward, it must remain one country, reassert its secular credentials and throw out communally based parties from the political arena.

What concerns me is how narrow-minded and intolerant we Indians have become.

What has been happening in Mumbai, what the Shiv Sena is doing, is anti-national. I lived in Mumbai for nine years without understanding or speaking Marathi. At no time was I made to feel I didn't belong. We are Indian first. To be parochial and reject people because they aren't from the same state or speak a different language is to be un-Indian. It is alarming to see educated people express views that don't reflect their liberal education. On the contrary, I have often found them to be the most bigoted, prejudiced, fanatic of them all.

If we love our country, we have to save it from communal forces. And though the liberal class is shrinking, I do hope that the present generation totally rejects communal and fascist policies.

MY WEAKNESSES AND INSECURITIES

My biggest weakness is my inability to say no. I know people, many women included, take advantage of me, yet I cannot say no. I don't get anything out of these people who take advantage of me—absolutely nothing. And the women, they just cuddle up to me or wrap their arms around me, give me a hug and a kiss and that's enough for me to feel good. Women have always behaved like this with me, even in front of my wife—they'd do it even when she was around. And it didn't upset her.

My insecurities show up in my dreams. I dream that I'm lost in a place and don't have any money. I think I have these dreams because there was a time when I had very little money and it was like that right until I took over as editor of *The Illustrated Weekly* and my books started getting published. My father had supported me then but that insecurity seems to have crept in.

ON WORK

It is work, my writing, that keeps me going. Writing is a solitary profession and you simply cannot write in a crowd or in the midst of people.

Over the years I have discovered what enormous energy silence creates, energy that socializing and useless chit chat depletes. You have got to train yourself to be alone. You have to discipline yourself to follow a slavish routine. As always, even to this day, I'm up early and the day begins with solving crossword puzzles and reading the newspapers. No matter what happens I don't let everyday tensions come in the way of my work and the deadlines I have for the day.

I jot down my deadlines for the day in the morning itself and don't retire till I have completed the day's work. This includes writing, from about three in the afternoon right until seven in the evening. And answering all the letters that I receive myself. I get around thirty letters every day and they come in four languages—Punjabi, English, Hindi, Urdu. Some of these are even abusive, calling me '*Pakistani randi ki aulad*' (son of a Pakistani prostitute) or calling me a Pakistani agent, but I see to it that I reply to even these, if the sender has sent me his address.

There's really no substitute for work. Years ago, when I was sixty-nine and in my third year as editor of *The Hindustan Times* and the contract had to be renewed, the proprietor, K.K. Birla, had asked me whether I had any plans to retire. I'd told him then, '*Birla-ji*, retire *toh Nigambodh Ghaat mein honga.*' (I will retire when I'm taken to the cremation grounds.)

I've never wasted a moment in prayers, nor in love affairs or relationships. They're such a

ON WORK

waste of time. I don't even watch cricket or tennis matches on TV anymore, not even these IPL matches. I have absolutely no interest in them. I don't know any of these new players and also all this money has taken away the fun.

ON BEING A WRITER

I have never taken anyone too seriously, least of all myself. I have always been a nosy person, forever probing into other people's private lives. I love to gossip and have an insatiable appetite for scandal. When I landed my first job as editor of *Yojana*, over fifty years ago, I discovered I could exploit these negative traits to my benefit. Readers were amused by what I wrote and asked for more. An editor of *The Times of India* had scoffed at me as he remarked, 'You have made bullshit an art form.' I was flattered.

I resumed my column when I took over as editor of *The Illustrated Weekly of India* in 1969. I wrote on subjects other editors considered

ON BEING A WRITER 51

beneath contempt. I wrote on why some monkeys have red bottoms, on the refined art of bottom pinching, shop lifting without getting caught, the joys of drinking, mocking politicians, godmen, astrologers and my favourite target—name droppers. Mario Miranda designed the logo that accompanied my column, of me in a bulb with a pile of books and a bottle of whiskey beside me. I use it even today. It has become my trademark.

Soon after I began my writing career, I took a conscious decision to write on specific subjects. Hardly any Sikh had written anything in English on Sikh history or Sikhism. I knew the Sikh morning prayer Japji by heart and translated it verse by verse. I wrote it down and had it published in London by Arthur Probsthain. It was an instant success and, thanks to the Sikh community, was a sell-out. Later, when I wrote *A History of the Sikhs*, I felt my life's work was done. It was my *opus exegi*. The two volumes were first published in 1963 and I dedicated them to my parents Sardar Bahadur

Sir Sobha Singh and Lady Viran Bai.

I have never rated myself very highly as a writer. I can tell good writing from the not-so-good and first-rate writing from the passable. I know that of Indian writers or those of Indian origin the late Nirad Chaudhuri, Naipaul, Rushdie, Amitava Ghosh and Vikram Seth handle the English language better than I. I also know that I can and have written as well as R.K. Narayan, Mulk Raj Anand, Malgaonkar, Ruth Jhabvala, Nayantara Sahgal and Anita Desai. Unlike most I have never claimed to be a great writer. Almost every Indian writer I have met lauds his or her achievements. You have to be born a writer. No school or classes can teach you how to become one. There has to be something in you. And you have to keep at it. You are lucky if you can write both fiction and non-fiction with equal ease and prowess. Writers have different styles and each writer is unique. They can be temperamental, have their quirks and eccentricities. They can be moody and dislikeable; they can be warm and kind human beings. Usually, writers are an interesting and colourful bunch—though I can think of a few who are crashing bores. Salman Rushdie is a great womanizer and has one relationship after another; Vikram Seth has openly declared that he is gay—he didn't have to publicize something that is so private—it was unnecessary; V.S. Naipaul's biography shows us a very ugly side of him. It's not about visiting prostitutes—lots of people go to prostitutes—there's nothing unusual in that. Maybe he didn't have the confidence to cultivate a friend. It's the way he treated his wife and mistress. It was terrible. I'd met both of them here in Delhi when they came to meet me and even took them out for dinners and went with them whenever I was invited. I'm not quite sure whether Naipaul approved of all this being written about in his biography, because he is a shy, aggressive man.

Two writers who had a huge impact on me when I was young were Aldous Huxley and Somerset Maugham. Their work left a deep and lasting impression on me. Amongst today's writers I admire several: Salman Rushdie—but only his earlier works—Vikram Seth, Amitav Ghosh and Arundhati Roy.

The world of writers and publishers has changed beyond recognition. The pioneers of Indians writing in English—Mulk Raj Anand, R.K. Narayan and Raja Rao either had patrons who helped them find publishers or organizations which sponsored their works. They made some noise in literary circles but not much money. Literary agents were little known. The only one I'd heard of then was Curtis Brown. It was said that if the agent took up your work, they would find you a good publisher and take their cut on royalties due to you. Today a literary agent has become a powerful factor in publishing: the best writers use them because it is the agents who get publishing houses to cough up huge sums as advance royalties. The whole business resembles a whorehouse. Publishers can be compared to brothel keepers, literary agents to *bharooahs* [pimps] who find eligible girls and fix rates of payment; writers can be likened to prostitutes. Newcomers are *naya maal* [virgins] who draw the biggest fees for being deflowered. I for one never went through a literary agent—nor did I have problems finding a good publisher. I was happy with the 8 to 10 per cent they gave me on the sales of my books.

I have often been asked how one becomes a good writer. I'd say that one has to slog and be totally honest and fearless. Always speak out. One might face problems, but one mustn't give in. Along with hard work, read whatever you can—whether it's classics or fairytales or even nonsense verse. Reading—reading as much as you can—will make you capable of distinguishing between bad and good writing.

Also, one should never be pretentious or have pretences; be honest and not show off by using difficult words. That comes in the way of communicating with the reader. Always do your homework. A writer's responsibility—whether you're an essayist or a novelist—is to inform your reader while you provoke or entertain him. The challenge is to tell your reader something he doesn't know. Don't talk down to the reader; level with him. Above all, don't be afraid to be yourself.

If you write fearlessly and candidly you have to be prepared to pay the price. And there's no point writing if you're not honest. It's because of my writing that I have got the reputation of being a dirty old man but it's never bothered me. I've always written what I felt and believed to be true. I bared all in my autobiography—if I hadn't it wouldn't have been honest, and there wouldn't have been any point in writing it.

If you write then you also have to be prepared for criticism. Every day I get several letters

ON BEING A WRITER 57

which are full of gaalis. Most accuse me of being pro-Muslim and an anti-Hindu, and this is mostly because I write against the communal cries of some political parties. I have even received death threats—when I wrote against Bhindranwale I was on the Khalistani hit list—but none of this has ever bothered me, really. I have never felt like giving it back to my critics, because I'm not vengeful. Not even when people I considered friends, people whom I have helped at various stages, have taken me to court. It's just not in me to take revenge.

My autobiography was a tell-all—I concealed nothing; there's no secret I kept to myself. I write what comes to my mind and at times this has upset people. I know I'm often misunderstood as a *sharabi-kababi* type because I write openly about my love for alcohol, women and four-letter words. But I've never been bothered by my reputation.

THOSE I RESPECT
AND ADMIRE

In the study in my cottage in Kasauli, I have two pictures of the people I admire most—Mahatma Gandhi and Mother Teresa.

I admire Bapu Gandhi more than any other man. Of all the other prophets of the past, we have no knowledge. Almost everything about them is myth or miracle. With Gandhi, we know—he walked among us not long ago and there are many people alive, like me, who have seen him. He was always in the public eye. He bared himself; no one was more honest.

I don't accept his foibles. He took a vow of celibacy in his prime, but without consulting

THOSE I RESPECT AND ADMIRE 59

his wife, which I think was grossly unfair. He would sleep naked beside young girls to test his brahmacharya. He could be very odd. But these are small matters. His insistence on truth at all times made him a Mahatma. And the principle of Ahimsa: not to hurt anyone. Ahimsa and honesty should be the basis of all religion, of every life.

I've been a regular drinker all my adult life. I celebrate sex and cannot say that I have never lied. I have not hurt anyone physically but I think I've caused hurt with my words and actions. And sometimes there is no forgiveness in me. But I consider myself a Gandhian. Whenever I feel unsure of anything, I try to imagine what Gandhi would have done and that is what I do.

I became a Gandhi bhakta at a young age. I first saw Bapu when I was six or seven years old, when I was studying in Modern School. He had come on a visit. All of us children—there were very few students in the school those days—sat on the ground in the front row.

He bent down and tugged my uniform playfully.

'*Beta, yeh kapda kahan ka hai?*' he asked.

'*Vilayati,*' I said with pride.

He told me gently, '*Yeh apne desh ka hota toh achha hota, nahin?*'

Soon after, I started wearing khadi. My mother used to spin khaddar, so it was easy. I continued wearing khaddar for many years. Before I went London to attend university, I took some khaddar to our tailor because I had been told I would need a proper English suit. The tailor laughed and told my father, who asked me to stop being a *khotta*!

It must have been more than thirty years ago that I was asked to do a profile of Mother Teresa for *The New York Times*. I wrote to Mother Teresa seeking her permission to call on her. Having got it, I spent three days with her, from the early hours of the morning to late at night. Nothing in my long journalistic

THOSE I RESPECT AND ADMIRE 61

career has remained as sharply etched in my memory as those three days with her in Calcutta.

Before I met her, I read Malcolm Muggeridge's book on her, *Something Beautiful for God*. Malcolm was a recent convert to Catholicism and prone to believe in miracles. He had gone to make a film on Mother Teresa for the British Broadcasting Corporation (BBC). They first went to the Nirmal Hriday (Sacred Heart) Home for dying destitutes close to the Kalighat temple. The team took some shots of the building from outside and if its sunlit courtyard. The camera crew was of the opinion that the interior was too dark, and they had no lights that would help them take the shots they needed. However, since some footage was left over, they decided to use it for interior shots. When the film was developed later, the shots of the dormitories inside were found to be clearer and brighter than those taken in sunlight. The first thing I asked Mother Teresa was if this was true. She replied, 'But of course.

Such things happen all the time.' And she added with greater intensity, 'Every day, every hour, every single minute, God manifests Himself in some miracle.' She narrated other miracles of the days when her organization was little known and always short of cash. 'Money has never been much of a problem,' she told me, 'God gives through His people.' She told me that when she started her first school in the slums, she had no more than five rupees with her. But as soon as people came to know what she was doing, they brought money and other things. The first institution she took me to was Nirmal Hriday. It was in 1952 that the Calcutta Corporation had handed the building over to her. Orthodox Hindus were outraged. Four hundred Brahmin priests attached to the Kali temple demonstrated outside the building. 'One day I went out and spoke to them, "If you want to kill me, kill me. But do not disturb the inmates. Let them die in peace." That silenced them. Then one of the priests staggered in. He was in an advanced stage of galloping phthisis.

THOSE I RESPECT AND ADMIRE 63

The nuns looked after him till he died.' That changed the priests' attitude towards Mother Teresa. Later, one day, another priest entered the Home, prostrated himself at Mother Teresa's feet and said, 'For thirty years I have served the Goddess Kali in her temple. Now the Goddess stands before me.'

On my way back, Mother Teresa dropped me at the Dum Dum Airport. As I was about to take leave of her she said, 'So?', wanting to know whether I had anything else to ask her. 'Tell me how can you touch people with loathsome diseases like leprosy and gangrene? Aren't you revolted by people filthy with dysentery and cholera vomit?' She replied, 'I see Jesus in every human being. I say to myself, this is hungry Jesus. This one has gangrene, dysentery or cholera. I must wash him and tend to him.'

I wrote a humble tribute to her for *The New York Times* and put her on the cover of *The Illustrated Weekly*. Till then she was little known outside Calcutta; after that more people got to know about her work. She sent me a short note of thanks which I have in a silver frame in Kasauli. It is among my most valued possessions: 'I am told you do not believe in God. I send you God's blessings.'

I have often thought about those three days I spent with Mother Teresa in Calcutta. We walked through crowded streets, rode in trams to visit her various hospitals, creches for abandoned children and homes for the dying. I still remember how she tended to a very ill man who was dying. She was with him, looking after him all the time telling him to say 'Bhogoban achhen' (There is God). The way in which Mother Teresa went about looking after and tending to the sick, the dying, the hungry—it was the same with Bhagat Puran Singh. I heard of his *pingalwara* in Amritsar and persuaded members of my family's charitable trust to donate some money for the inmates there.

Some years later, during one of my trips to Calcutta, I'd asked her to meet me but she declined, saying that she wouldn't come to my hotel room. It was okay by me, because I respected her. I saw her last when she was in Delhi. She had come here when H.S. Sikand (of Sikand Motors) had gifted a van for her Missionaries of Charity, but this time she didn't seem to recognize me. I'd smiled and greeted her and though she did smile back, she did so in the way you do when you don't really recognize the person.

There are not too many people I am in awe of. The most knowledgeable person I've known was Nirad C. Chaudhuri. I haven't come across any person with such deep knowledge of just about anything.

Nirad was a small, frail man, a little over five feet, who led a double life. At home he dressed in dhoti-kurta and sat on the floor to do his reading and writing. When he left for work, he wore European dress: coat, tie, trousers and a monstrous sola topi. Nirad babu was not a

66 ABSOLUTE KHUSHWANT

modest man. But he had great reason to be immodest. No Indian, living or dead, wrote the English language as well as he did.

Nirad had written in Bengali for many years. But it was not until his first book in English, *The Autobiography of an Unknown Indian*, was published, that he really aroused the interest of the class to which he belonged and which, because of the years of indifference to him, he had come to loathe—the Anglicized upper middle class of India. This class of people was more English than Indian but proclaimed their patriotism at the expense of the British. Having lost their own traditions and not having fully imbibed those of England, they were a breed with pretensions to intellectualism. He dedicated the book 'To the British Empire . . .' People in India took the bait and sent up a howl of protest. However, many discovered to their surprise that there was nothing anti-Indian in the book. On the contrary, it was the most beautiful picture of East Bengal (where Nirad was born and spent his childhood) that anyone

THOSE I RESPECT AND ADMIRE 67

had ever painted. And India had produced a writer who could write the English language as it should be written—and as few, if any, living Englishmen could write.

Nobody could afford to ignore Nirad Chaudhuri any more. He and his wife Amiya became the most sought-after couple in Delhi's upper-class circles. Anecdotes of his vast fund of knowledge were favourite topics at dinner parties. Nirad babu could talk about any subject under the sun. There was not a bird, tree, butterfly or insect whose name he did not know in Latin, Sanskrit, Hindi and Bengali. He also had a phenomenal memory. Long before he left for London, he not only knew where the important monuments and museums were, but also the location of many famous restaurants. I'd heard him discuss stars with astronomers, recite lines from obscure fifteenth century French literature, and advise a wine dealer on the best vintages from Burgundy.

If Nirad was immodest, he could also be very angry. And he had much to be angry about.

ABSOLUTE KHUSHWANT

The Government of India had issued a fiat to its various departments not to publish anything by him. He was dismissed from service as political commentator on All India Radio by the half-baked I&B Minister Dr B.V. Keskar, because the Government prohibited employees from publishing memoirs. With his job gone and three growing boys, life was hard for the Chaudhuris. Years later, when the Government of India wanted him to write a series of articles on the plight of the Hindu minority in East Pakistan and offered him a blank cheque, he refused, in spite of his financial plight. When I conveyed Finance Minister T.T. Krishnamachari's proposal to him, he told me, 'The Government may have lifted its ban on Nirad Chaudhuri, but Nirad Chaudhuri has not lifted his ban on the Government of India.'

Life in Oxford was difficult for Nirad in his last years. It was not easy living on his royalties. When I wrote about this in my column, K.K. Birla sent me a letter asking me to tell

Nirad babu that he would be happy to give him a stipend for life for any amount in any currency he wanted. When I sent Nirad Mr Birla's letter, he wrote back asking me to thank Birla for his generous offer, but refused to accept it. However, he did accept a CBE from the British Government, though it was a peerage he deserved because he was genuinely a peerless man of intellect and letters.

I believe Manmohan [Singh] is the best prime minister we have had. I would even rate him higher than Nehru. Nehru had vision and charisma, but he had his faults. He was instinctively anti-American and blindly pro-Soviet and socialist. He could also be impatient with people and had favourites. Manmohan has a free and extremely good mind. He can't be accused of nepotism. Nehru could, Indira could. No one would say that of Manmohan Singh.

He had the courage to disagree with Nehru's

socialist vision and turn away from Mrs Gandhi's legacy. He pursued a pro-America policy. He opened India to the world, championed the private sector and set us on the path of economic progress without compromising India's interests. He has completely turned around our sick economy.

He is also very humble and simple. He grew up in a small village in a family of very modest means and struggled to get an education. Initially his ambition was only to be a college professor, find a small flat and settle in Chandigarh. Then chance changed the course of his life and took him to Cambridge and Oxford, the UN and the highest positions in India's financial institutions; and now he is prime minister. But he remained grounded.

I really got to know him at the election he lost from South Delhi. This was in 1999. I was surprised and impressed because his son-in-law, whom my family knew, came to borrow some money—just two lakhs—to hire taxis that were needed for the campaigning. They didn't even have that much to spare! I gave the money, in cash.

Only days after he had lost the election, Manmohan Singh called me himself and asked for an appointment. He came to see me with a packet. 'I haven't used the money,' he said and handed me the packet with all the cash I had given his son-in-law. That kind of thing no politician would do!

When people talk of integrity, I say the best example is the man who occupies the country's highest office.

Two people who have had a great impact on me are my Urdu teacher Maulvi Shafiuddin Nayar at the Modern School and Manzoor Qadir, my lawyer-friend in Lahore. Two of the finest human beings, they left a deep impression on me and influenced me greatly. And it's probably because of my teacher, Manzoor and Ghayoor that I have such a special fondness for Muslims.

JAWAHARLAL NEHRU

Nehru answered Allama Iqbal's requirements of a Meer-e-Kaarvaan—leader of the caravan: '*Nigah buland, sukhan dilnawaz, jaan par soz/ Yahi hain rakht-e-safar Meer-e-Kaarvaan ke liye*' (Lofty vision, winning speech and a warm personality/This is all the baggage the leader of a caravan needs on his journey).

He should have been the role model for the prime ministers of India. He was above prejudices of any kind: racial, religious or of caste. He was an agnostic and firmly believed that religion played a very negative role in Indian society. What I admired most about him was his secularism. He was a visionary and an exemplary leader; the father of Indian constitutional democracy, of universal adult franchise, the five-year plans, giving equal rights to women, among other things. He was better educated than any of his successors, with the exception of Manmohan Singh, and spent nine long years in jail reading, writing and thinking about the country's future.

But being human, Nehru had his human failings. He was not above political chicanery. Having accepted the Cabinet Mission plan to hand over power to a united India, he reneged on his undertaking when he realized Jinnah might end up becoming prime minister.

He had blind spots too. He refused to believe that India's exploding population needed to be contained. He refused to see the gathering strength of Muslim separatism which led to the formation of Pakistan. He failed to come to terms with Pakistan and was chiefly responsible for the mess we made in Jammu and Kashmir.

He was also given to nepotism and favouritism.

ABSOLUTE KHUSHWANT

I first met Nehru in London, when I was a Press Officer at the Indian Embassy, and my first impression of him was that he was short-tempered. He could also be ill-mannered.

I once had to host a lunch so that the editors of leading British newspapers could meet him. Halfway through the meal, Nehru fell silent. When questions were put to him he looked up at the ceiling and did not reply. He proceeded to light a cigarette while others were still eating. To make matters worse, Krishna Menon fell asleep. It was a disastrous attempt at public relations.

Another time, he arrived in London past midnight. I asked Nehru whether he would like me to accompany him to his hotel. 'Don't be silly,' he said. 'Go home and sleep.' The next morning one of the papers had a photo of him with Lady Mountbatten opening the door in her negligee. The huge caption read: Lady Mountbatten's Midnight Visitor. Nehru was furious. On another occasion, he'd taken Lady Mountbatten for a quiet dinner at a Greek restaurant. Once again the following morning's papers carried photographs of them sitting close to each other. When I was summoned, Nehru asked, 'Who are you?' 'I'm your PRO in London, Sir,' I replied. 'You have a strange notion of publicity,' Nehru said curtly.

I thought it best to remain silent.

INDIRA GANDHI

I first met Indira Gandhi in Lahore when I must have been around eighteen. She was very young and looked very shy and, if I remember correctly, she had come with Kitchlew [Saifuddin]. Years later, when I met her again in Delhi, she didn't remember our first meeting.

There were many who were bowled over by Mrs Gandhi's looks. I found her good-looking in a cold, haughty sort of way.

She never forgave anyone who said anything negative about her. She never forgave her aunt Vijayalakshmi Pandit—or her daughters, for that matter—for making derogatory remarks about her looks and her intelligence. She was also

INDIRA GANDHI

touchy about her health. She had been suspected of having tuberculosis when she was a girl and doctors had advised her not to have children. 'If it had been up to me,' she'd said, 'I would have had eleven.' To prove her doctors wrong she rode on horseback, on elephants and walked vast distances, maintaining punishing schedules. 'Tiredness is a state of mind, not of the body,' she would say.

Those who described her as a 'goongi gudiya' or a 'chhokree' were wide off the mark. She was dictatorial and, like her father, indulged in favouritism. She overlooked corruption and undermined democratic institutions. She manipulated and gagged the press. And she wanted dynastic succession. Power went to her head. This is why her public image changed from goddess to vindictive despot.

I know the majority of Indians feel that Indira Gandhi was the strongest leader we have ever had. They see her as Durga. There was a reason why they called her the only man in her cabinet. She certainly knew how to use power and appeal to huge crowds at her election rallies. But my instincts are against her.

She was stern, severe and cold, and would impose her wishes on people, often wrongly. Mrs Gandhi had very strong likes and dislikes. She could be vengeful, extremely critical and even petty. She had many shortcomings; I suppose it was these that made her human. But what I found most disturbing about her was that she could be rude and vindictive towards even those who were close to her. I think it was because she was very insecure. I learned that soon after I got to know her, and then I kept my distance.

I was never close to Mrs Gandhi, though I'd met her several times. On a few occasions my wife and I had invited the family over for dinner and they'd accepted our invitation. She came to our home often when she was out of power after the Emergency, sometimes with Sonia or Maneka. Later, when she was having trouble with Maneka, she'd even sent for me and told me to talk to her, to tell her to behave

INDIRA GANDHI

herself. But in the years that followed, when relations really soured between them, Mrs Gandhi thought I was supporting Maneka. When I tried telling her this was not true at all, she just wouldn't believe me. I decided after that, to stay away from both of them, and avoided meeting either. She never visited us after she returned to power. And much later, when Mrs Gandhi invited me on two or three occasions, for some function or the other, I didn't go.

But when she was assassinated I felt shock. I was upset, because I had made an equation with her despite difficulties and differences. She had been foolish and bungled badly in Punjab. She had made enemies. But she did not deserve the kind of death she had. It was a sad day.

You can't doubt Mrs Gandhi's patriotism. And I can vouch that there was nothing anti-Sikh about her. On Blue Star she was misled by her advisers, one of them a Mona sardar!

She surrounded herself with very suspect and cynical advisers. She was also very tolerant of corruption. She may not have been corrupt herself, but the suitcase culture and massive corruption started in her time. She took no action. She did great harm to the country.

Indira Gandhi's greatest moment was the Bangladesh war. She did it with great skill, by deftly isolating Pakistan and supporting our armed forces completely. She backed the right people. The world was rightly impressed when she stood up to American pressure and would not be intimidated by American warships in the Indian Ocean. It was all over very quickly. Maybe she would have given in if the war had lasted more than a few days.

But more than the war, her biggest achievement was how the country responded to the refugees from East Pakistan. Millions of refugees were given shelter, food and medicines. We were a poor country but they were all taken care of. The Bangladeshis now won't acknowledge Indira Gandhi's or India's role in their history. Everything begins and ends with Mukti Bahini. That is not true. They have a lot to thank Indira Gandhi for.

SANJAY AND VARUN GANDHI

I met Sanjay in the mid 1970s and found him to be reasonable and courteous. He was the one who called the meeting. He wanted to talk to me about his Maruti car business and wanted me to write about it. I went with him to the factory site. I was disappointed; it looked like the workshop of a *lohar*. I was not impressed. He drove around the site, driving fast and talking about how important the project was.

It was being said that Bansi Lal had given Sanjay land for free for his factory. I found these allegations to be false. Sanjay had paid a fair price. I wrote this in my story on Maruti. That was how our association began.

82   ABSOLUTE KHUSHWANT

I have been criticized for supporting Sanjay and his mother and the Emergency she'd imposed. I don't deny that I supported them and I have no regrets. Even now, after all these years, I think it was necessary at the time. I had no idea then that it could and would be misused and abused. Sanjay was always extremely courteous to me. When I first met him, he really did seem like a committed man. The opposition had unleashed chaos. Nothing in the country functioned, and he appeared to be a no-nonsense man who liked to get things done. But a year or so into the Emergency he had become dictatorial and very unpopular because of the forced *nasbandi* programme and censorship.

Maneka and her family used and exploited me. I think she's a no-good politician but Sanjay, I must say, was always true to his word. He had a conscience. And he was a man of action. He was a doer and was impatient to bring about changes. Many said he had the makings of a dictator—because of the demolition drives that razed slums to the ground overnight and the family planning methods he forced on people—but I feel that he was keen to bring about rapid changes. He had a vision and this was not really understood.

Sanjay came to see me in Bombay shortly after the Emergency. There were mobs in the streets baying for his blood. I had to drive him to the airport at some risk.

If he had lived, this country would not have been a democracy. There would have been order and much faster development, but no democracy, of that I am sure. Would I still have supported him? Oh, I don't know. He would probably have got around me. He could be a real charmer. He had been good to me. He put me in Parliament. Even *The Hindustan Times*—it was he who called up Birla and told him to give me the editor's job!

Varun should never have been allowed to contest in the recent elections. He should have been banned from contesting and people should have had the sense to keep him out. Such men are dangerous for the very unity of the country. His abusive language and the venom he spilled against Muslims showed his very poor upbringing. It's shocking, because if we have politicians of this sort—who openly abuse Muslims from public platforms—you can well imagine the future of the country. What also worries me is that many others speak with the same venom [as he did] against the minorities of this country. The only difference is that they confine their hatred to their drawing rooms.

Maneka had invited me to launch Varun's collection of poetry some years ago, and I'd accepted. I had read his poems, liked them and given the collection a favourable write-up. I thought a young man who was into poetry would be above dirty politics. I was wrong.

The language Varun used on that platform was the language of the gutter which is absolutely unpardonable. It made me wonder when such anti-Muslim sentiments entered the boy's mind. During his grandmother's time a permanent fixture in their home was a Muslim, Mohammed Yunus. Both his parents called him 'Chacha Yunus'. They were married in his house on Tughlak Road. I never heard Sanjay or any other member of the Gandhi family use derogatory words for Muslims. The term *bara bajey* for a Sikh is even harder to understand. In short, Varun Gandhi has, as the saying goes, cooked his own goose.

RAJIV AND RAHUL GANDHI

We tend to build a legend around Rajiv Gandhi, glorifying him. But Rajiv had made more than a couple of mistakes in his time, call them grave errors of judgement if you will.

Rajiv was bullied into a position he wasn't equipped to handle. He was pleasant enough, and had some good ideas, but none of them extraordinary. He wasn't really a leader. And I don't think he was cut out for politics. He followed in his mother's footsteps and made many of the same mistakes. Even the positive things he did, like telecom and computers—the plans had started in Indira Gandhi's time. He bungled in Sri Lanka; he even fired a minister

RAJIV AND RAHUL GANDHI

at a public conference! His role in both the Shah Bano case and in the Babri Masjid incident cannot be denied. Both were big blunders that were irreversible and did long-term damage.

Rajiv was young and charming, so the country was optimistic when he came to power. But he did very little with the massive mandate he had won after his mother's assassination.

History will never forget the shameful way in which he behaved after Mrs Gandhi died. That speech he made: 'When a big tree falls, the earth is bound to shake . . .' when Sikhs were being burnt alive in the capital—that was unforgivable! He could easily have stopped the massacres. All he had to do was go out and say, 'This must stop' and call in the army. But he didn't, he almost justified the carnage with that remark. I cannot imagine his grandfather [Nehru] allowing such a thing to continue. Nehru had courage; he would have gone out and confronted the mobs. He did that during the Partition riots. That's the difference between a leader and a novice.

Sanjay was dynamic; Rajiv was just a boy scout.

I think Rahul is much more talented than his father. He has a vision and that's very important. I'm impressed with him, impressed with the way in which he's conducting himself. He has the right attitude. Even if much of what he does only amounts to gestures, the thinking behind them is right.

He has taken on Mayawati in her own territory. It is a brave thing to do. He himself seems to have no caste or class prejudice. What he has been doing in Amethi, staying with the lowest castes and sharing their food—I don't think you can criticize him for that. He is not being patronizing; he is highlighting a shameful reality in our country. Even in the twenty-first century there are untouchables in our society and they live wretched lives.

And the manner in which he took on the

RAJIV AND RAHUL GANDHI

Shiv Sena in Bombay [February 2010]. He lambasted them for attacking non-Maharashtrians and said publicly that Bombay was for all Indians. Then he went to the lion's den and dared them to do their worst. He walked around in the streets, travelled by local train. The Shiv Sena goondas failed completely. Hardly any Maharashtrian joined the Shiv Sena protest against Rahul. It was a very well-planned move by Rahul and his advisers. It was good theatre.

The young Gandhi is becoming a mature leader. Maybe after the next elections [2014], if his party wins, he may agree to become PM. Or he may still choose not to. He has his priorities right—he is not concerned about position and *kursi*, but strengthening the Congress party.

Rahul had telephoned sometime last year and said that he wanted to come and see me. He came at the appointed time—4 p.m.—and spent almost an hour in my home. I gave him tea—he said he'd like some tea—and we spoke of politics; about the current situation in general and other things in particular.

I told him, 'Your cadres are very weak. The BJP has the RSS and VHP to work for it at the grassroots level. The Congress lacks that.' He said he agreed with me and that he was already working on this. He is seeing to it that party members are trained and the party built up. I see that he has been concentrating on young workers and has picked some very talented youngsters, many of them women. I also told him that during elections, voters have to be wooed and drawn towards the party. I said that the most important thing that he should keep in mind is to resist flatterers and to hold back from accepting any portfolio.

We didn't talk about his grandmother or his great grandfather.

ON HONESTY

I don't think there are many honest people around these days. I can't think of anyone. My ideal in this regard will always be Manzur Qadir, whom I had first met while practising at the Lahore High Court. Later, he became Pakistan's foreign minister and then chief justice of the Lahore High Court. In all these years I haven't met a more honest man than Qadir and that's why I keep his photograph on my mantelpiece, where I can always see it. Qadir was so honest that the income-tax department had invariably to return money to him for he always overpaid. He was the only person I know who never told a lie and took great pains

ABSOLUTE KHUSHWANT

to avoid hurting people. He was a sort of litmus paper with which his friends would test their own integrity. Whenever we were in doubt about what would be the right thing to do, we'd ask ourselves, would Manzur approve?

Manzur was most unusual. He observed the highest standards of rectitude, a rare trait, particularly among lawyers. He took his fees by cheque and when someone did pay in cash, gave receipts for the full amount.

A couple of years older than me, Manzur and I shared a love for literature. And like me, he was an agnostic. A short, balding man with thick glasses, Manzur married Asghari, a great beauty, whom the painter Roerich used as a model for his portraits of the Madonna. Manzur and I were lucky that our wives, both equally difficult, hit it off. We began eating in each other's homes every other evening. Kaval shared Manzur's enthusiasm for the cinema and went to the movies together at least once every week. They also shared a passion for mangoes and would, between them, demolish a dozen at one

ON HONESTY

sitting. Our friendship was much talked about, especially since such close friendships between Sikhs or Hindus and Muslims were rare in those days.

Honesty is such a rare virtue these days that awards are given to people for being honest. Sulabh International had conferred the 'Honest Man of the Year' award on me in 2000. I'm sure there are hundreds of honest people around but if I'm asked to point them out I'd have great difficulty in doing so.

There are no set yardsticks to measure honesty, but I could safely say one thing about myself—I have rarely ever lied and this has been so right from my childhood. I have always been outspoken and written without fear of any kind. I've never lied to my wife or to my friends. This may be because I'm emotionally strong. I have never cultivated a close friend or lover. I could be dropped by friends but I'm least bothered. I have always been fearless, even as a child I was known to speak my mind. Of course, there are consequences. I was on the hit list of a certain terrorist group and my house had to be guarded for fifteen years, so there are ways in which I've had to pay a price.

It is tragic that a clean man like Manmohan Singh can lose in an election whereas Phoolan Devi won. We've had ministers in the Centre—Murli Manohar Joshi and L.K. Advani—who've faced a chargesheet and yet continued to hold on to their portfolios. This alone speaks volumes. The situation is really pathetic; it cannot get worse. I drown my sorrow in a glass of whisky every evening and I feel ashamed. The average man withdraws into himself but he shouldn't become bitter, for bitterness erodes one's being.

ON THE BRITISH

I think the happiest phase of my life was when I was studying in England. I was carefree, and I had many friends.

Indians have looked upon the English as unwanted rulers who exploited India, kept their distance from Indians and, as soon as tenures were over, went back to their homes in England. All victorious armies plunder, rape and kill. Some go on a rampage without the slightest concern about public opinion. The truth is that the British did it with finesse and more thoroughness than the others. It was during my years in London as a student and then with our High Commission that I saw some of the loot that the British had taken from the Punjab. There was of course the Koh-i-Noor diamond taken from the boy Maharaja Dalip Singh, youngest son of Maharaja Ranjit Singh. It was also cut into three—one piece each for the crowns of the King and Queen of England and one piece on display at the Tower of London museum. There was Ranjit Singh's gold-leaf covered throne in the Victoria and Albert Museum. There were innumerable weapons—cannons, muskets, swords, spears, shields and chainmail shirts in the War Museum. Manuscripts, documents, miniature paintings, scriptural texts, ceremonial robes . . . you name them, they had them, looted from all parts of India while they expanded their empire from the Arakan to the Indus. More than what could be seen were priceless artefacts taken by Governor Generals, army commanders, residents and senior civil servants. They were in private collections in castles and country mansions, now divided between descendants of the plunderers. And there is

ON THE BRITISH

97

little hope of our ever getting any of these back to our country, where they rightfully belong.

It is true that the majority of the British who came here came because they could not get good jobs in their own country. Many of them hated everything about India—its climate, the mosquitoes and flies, the dirt, the smell ... Above all, they hated Indians. There were others who enjoyed the luxury of living in spacious bungalows with a retinue of servants, shikar, horse-riding, pig-sticking, drinking and dancing, but kept to themselves, not mixing or socializing with Indians. They had 'white only' clubs and many of them remained aloof; some even made their disdain apparent. I clearly remember seeing a specially reserved train compartment at the Delhi railway station—it had a board with ONLY FOR EUROPEANS AND ANGLO-INDIANS on it. However, there was a third variety of the English race who liked everything about India. They looked down on these racist clubs and their fellow Englishmen who kept apart, and went out of their way to befriend Indians. They maintained contact with their Indian friends even after returning to England. I was fortunate to have known quite a few of this kind—both those I met and became friends with during my long years in England and those I got to know in India. Amongst those closest to me were the Sinclairs. Sinbad was head of Burmah Shell. When in Bombay, I never stayed in a hotel—it was always with Elinor Sinclair and her family. Later, whenever I was in England, the Sinclairs' home in London was my home. After Sinbad and Elinor died, it was the Croom-Johnsons. Henry was head of the British Council; his wife, Jane, a tall, handsome grey-eyed blonde, made it a point to reach out to Indians. She stayed with me in Kasauli, and my daughter and I stayed with her in London. Now Henry and Jane are also gone. But their children continue to be in touch with me and are friendly with Rahul and Mala, my son and daughter.

ON DELHI

Among the capitals of the world, Delhi is unique. It has a longer history and more historical monuments than any other metropolis. Relics discovered in and around the city date well beyond the sixth century BC. As for monuments, there are more mosques, mausolea and memorials in Delhi than in any city in a Muslim country. There are few mosques anywhere in the world that can rival Delhi's Jama Masjid. Another mosque that remains in your mind is the Moti Masjid or Pearl Mosque in the Red Fort, as small as the Jama Masjid is big. The beauty and perfection of Humayun's mausoleum made it the model for the Taj Mahal. Delhi has many exquisite modern buildings as well—the Rashtrapati Bhavan, the Secretariats, Parliament House, India Gate.

The river Yamuna, second only to the Ganga in sacredness, marked Delhi's eastern boundary, and a rocky ridge, the end of the Aravalli range, its western end. Between the river and the ridge rose several cities, each one the seat of the empire of Hindustan. As its population multiplied and spilled over the river and the ridge, Delhi became, after Calcutta and Bombay, the largest city of India.

Most of Delhi's trees grow wild, but a succession of rulers also laid out gardens and orchards wherever they lived. Little remains of these gardens today, besides their names: Hayat Baksh, Qudsia, Roshanara, Mahaldar Khan, among others. The most significant contribution was made by the British when they included extensive planting of trees in their blueprint for New Delhi. Saplings were planted as roads were laid out—the massive, shade-giving banyans, neems, jamuns, arjuns, mahuas and maulsaris that line the avenues of central Delhi. And, after Independence, the quick-growing jacarandas, laburnums, gulmohars and eucalypti. Between the old and the new, there is not a season when some tree or the other is not in full flower. The year starts with the glorious semul (silk cotton), followed by the chorisia (silk floss), palaash (flame of the forest), amaltas (laburnum), gulmohars and jarul (lagerstroenia). The city's greenery contributed to a rich bird life but much has changed. You don't see many mynahs and parakeets any more and sparrows have become scarce.

There was a time when Dilliwalas were known for their courteous speech, good food and clothes, and their interest in poetry—after all it was the city that produced Mir Taqi Mir, Ghalib, Zauq and Zafar. But all that went when the Muslim elite migrated to Pakistan in '47. They were replaced by Sikh and Hindu refugees from West Punjab eager to rehabilitate themselves, make a quick buck and show everyone how well they had done. Ostentatious display of wealth became the culture of Delhi's rich. And since the city is essentially one of babus and politicians, a caste system evolved quickly. A caste hierarchy of the bureaucracy where you are judged by your status in the civil service—and politicians have their own ways and means of letting people know how important they are.

You can love Delhi or hate it, but you cannot be indifferent towards it. My attitude towards the city cannot be clearly defined. Ghalib said it better: I asked my soul 'What is Delhi?' and my soul replied 'The world is the body, Delhi its life.'

With Jasjeet Singh and E.N. Mangat Rai (extreme right), college students in England.

With my college mates, King's College, London.

My parents (seated) *in Kasauli.*

Kaval and I on our wedding day.

Kaval and I.

Kaval and I on a picnic with Mrs Sheila Bharat Ram.

With Manzur and his wife Asghari.

Kaval and Rahul.

Kaval with Mala.

Rahul and Mala.

Feeding pigeons at Trafalgar Square, London, with Kaval and Mala.

With our son-in-law Ravi Dayal.

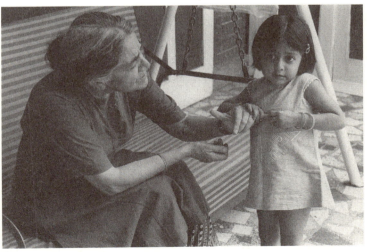

Kaval and my only grandchild Naina, the apple of our eye.

Krishna Menon, the Indian High Commissioner in London, with his Press Officer.

The first Commonwealth Prime Ministers' Conference, London.

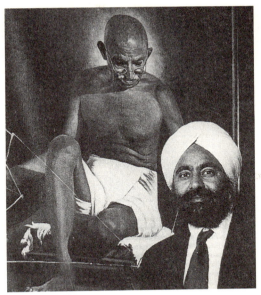

A portrait of Gandhi, true prophet and my role model.

Mother Teresa, the only woman I have admired.

With Sanjay Gandhi, whom I admired and owe a lot to.

Interviewing President Zia-ul Haq shortly after Bhutto was hanged.

With S. Radhakrishnan and M.S. Randawa.

With Giani Zail Singh when he was President of India.

Our house in Kasauli, Raj Villa, named after my mother-in-law.

Watching television at home, Sujan Singh Park.

ON DELHI

I started by loving Delhi and continued to love the city for many years. Then my passion began to wane. I have often resented living here, but since I have to spend the rest of my days in Delhi, I have had to make my peace with the city, come to terms with it.

I have always wanted people to love Delhi as much as I do. I have learnt much about the city roaming amongst its ancient ruins, its congested bazaars, mingling with its diplomatic corps and attending cocktail parties and I've always wanted to share all that I've learnt, so that people know about this city that I hold so dear. In my writing, through my novel *Delhi* and my columns, I have tried telling the story of Delhi from its earliest beginnings to the present times.

I began to get disenchanted by the city on 15 August 1947, the day of India's independence. My disenchantment had nothing to do with the British leaving our country but with what our new rulers did to the city I loved. Muslims who formed almost half the population of

104 ABSOLUTE KHUSHWANT

Delhi were forced out of the city, thanks to Partition. They took Urdu with them and the city's rich cultural life. The British had carefully planned New Delhi for a limited population. They left old monuments untouched. Independent India's new rulers did not have time to plan for the future. Huge parts of the old city wall were pulled down to make way for bazaars. New colonies sprang up everywhere, smothering ancient monuments—our new rulers did not believe these were worth preserving. It was heartbreaking. More than roads perpetually clogged by vehicles of all sorts, it is the murder of some of our past heritage that saddens me most.

I rarely go out these days. The last time I stepped out was to visit the dentist last year. But apart from bad traffic and many more cars on the road, I found the streets of Delhi haven't changed much. In fact, the city looked greener in some parts and cleaner.

ON PARTITION

Just as world history is divided into two distinct eras—BC (Before Christ) and AD (*Anno Domini*, 'in the year of our Lord'), for millions living in the Indian subcontinent, it is divided into BP (Before Partition) and PP (Post Partition).

15 August 1947 marked the divisive moment when Pakistan in the north-west and Pakistan in the east, which later became Bangladesh, were separated from India. In fact, long before Jinnah had come up with the two-nation theory, it was people like Keshav Baliram Hedgewar, Bal Gangadhar Tilak, Lajpat Rai and V.D. Savarkar who had come up with the Hindu-nation theory. Lajpat Rai had even drawn a map of divided India, dividing the

country into two parts along religious lines. It was a botched-up surgical operation. India's arms were chopped off without any anaesthesia, and streams of blood flooded the land of the five rivers known as the Punjab.

War broke out between Muslims on the one side, and Hindus and Sikhs on the other. It was not like other wars in which armed men battle with each other, but one in which one side, armed with swords, knives and staves, slew the other side, unarmed and unresisting. Over ten million were uprooted from their homes. In a couple of months a million were slaughtered in cold blood. Almost overnight, Muslims, Hindus and Sikhs, who had co-existed amicably over centuries, became sworn enemies.

The aftermath was more barbaric than anything beasts could have done to each other.

From March 1947 the exodus had begun. The two communities had already started moving and by April riots had broken. By August it was a full-fledged movement.

I was in Lahore till the 6th or 7th of August. There was a Parsi home near ours which had

ON PARTITION

107

'Parsee ka Makaan' scrawled on its boundary walls. A Christian home had put up the cross on their front gates. But I'd stayed on with Kaval and the children. In fact, Jinnah, who was very close to my father, had told him that I could stay on in Lahore and he'd also told my father that he'd make me a judge at the Lahore High Court. So I stayed on even though there was an apparent air of tension. Then, one day, the CID Chief—a British named Chris Everett who had studied with me in London—came over and told me that it was dangerous for me to stay there any longer. So I sent the children to their grandparents in Kasauli and, escorted by six Baluch constables, my wife and I took a train to Kalka.

As Kaval and I were heading towards the railway station we met Manzur Qadir. I handed him the keys to our home. We were sure that once the tension settled down we'd come back. That was not to be.

We first reached Kasauli and from there I drove to Delhi. There wasn't a soul in sight on the 200-mile stretch. I drove non-stop carrying a pistol with me—I didn't even know how to fire one. I realized then that things were not okay.

I arrived in Delhi on August 13, 1947. The next night I was among the crowd outside Parliament House, chanting *Bharat Mata ki jai*. We heard Sucheta Kripalani's voice over loudspeakers singing *Vande Mataram*; then Nehru's 'Tryst with Destiny' speech.

When my wife and I realized we could never go back, Manzur Qadir took great pains to have all our household things delivered to us—these included even half-empty whisky bottles—he had them sent across the border through a man named Bhagwan Das, a sessions judge at Ferozepur. This man drank the whisky and sent the furniture and other items. Two or three of my books, part of my prized collection, the then establishment in Pakistan did not allow to be sent across were Chughtai's translation of Ghalib's verse and an encyclopaedia of Islam (a Dutch publication).

ON PARTITION

India was never integrated. There was no real meeting of hearts between Hindus and Muslims. They have been friends but mostly on a superficial level. There was no real intermingling, no inter-community marriages. Jinnah harped on about Muslims being apprehensive of living in a Hindu-majority state and the majority of the Muslim middle class responded to this.

Partition was inevitable. It had to take place. Pointing fingers at any one or the whole bunch of political figures involved serves no purpose because nobody could have stopped it. The build-up, that fury, the communally charged atmosphere was difficult to control. The only thing is that Partition could have taken place without so much bloodshed and violence. It was the bloodiest exchange. I don't think either Pandit Nehru or Jinnah had imagined this level of violence. In any case both of them seemed to live in a dream world of their own— Jinnah had even hoped that he would go back to Bombay and live in his house there.

The only person who did seem to comprehend the very seriousness of Partition and all that followed was Mahatma Gandhi. He did not take part in any of the independence celebrations. He'd remained quiet and even went on a fast. When anti-Pakistan feelings were at a fever pitch and the Indian Government refused to honour its pledge to pay Pakistan Rs 55 crore, he went on a fast, forcing Patel and Nehru to keep their word. He knew he was asking for trouble but he did not give it a second thought. He told his secretary Pyarelal: 'Today I find myself alone. Even the Sardar [Patel] and Jawaharlal Nehru think that my reading of the situation is wrong and peace is sure to return if the Partition is agreed upon . . . I shall perhaps not be alive to witness it, but should the evil I apprehend overtake India and her independence be imperilled, let it not be said that Gandhi was a party to India's vivisection'.

ON THE 1984 RIOTS

I was witness to the Sikh riots in Delhi. I saw the police doing little to control the rioters. Journalists and activists who recounted the carnage in Gujarat, had similar stories to tell. When the police are given instructions to stand by and do nothing, it is time to be worried.

Delhi witnessed a bloodbath on 31 October 1984. 3000 Sikhs were killed in the capital Delhi alone and their property worth crores looted. Gurdwaras were burnt down and this massacre went uncontrolled. The government, the police, the establishment, did nothing.

I remember the day vividly. Around 11 in the morning I heard Mrs Gandhi had been

112   ABSOLUTE KHUSHWANT

shot in her house and had been taken to hospital. By the afternoon, I heard on the BBC that she was dead. For a couple of hours life in Delhi came to a standstill. Then all hell broke loose. Mobs yelling *'khoon ka badla khoon se lenge'* (we will avenge blood with blood) could be heard on the streets. Ordinary Sikhs going about their life were waylaid and roughed up. I saw a cloud of black smoke billowing up from Connaught Circus: Sikh-owned shops had been set on fire. I saw mobs smashing taxis owned by Sikhs right opposite my apartment. Sikh-owned shops in Khan market were looted. Over 100 policemen armed with lathis who lined the road did nothing. I saw them turn a blind eye. At midnight truckloads of men armed with cans of petrol attacked the gurdwara behind our house. The granthi was beaten up the men set fire to the shrine. Early next morning I rang up President Zail Singh. He would not take the call. His secretary told me that the President advised me to move into the home of a Hindu friend till the trouble was

ON THE 1984 RIOTS

over. The newly appointed prime minister Rajiv Gandhi was busy receiving guests arriving for his mother's funeral; Home Minister Narasimha Rao did not budge from his office; the Lt Governor had received no orders to take action against the rioters. Seventy-two gurdwaras were torched and thousands of Sikh homes looted. Around mid morning, a Swedish diplomat came in his car and took my wife and me to his home in the diplomatic enclave. Romesh Thapar had asked him to ensure we were safe. We had never met him before, but he kept us in his house for three days. I felt like a Jew must have in Nazi Germany; like a refugee in my own country. I began to understand how a Muslim might feel in a Hindu neighbourhood in a riot.

Later, I was pained to see names like Kamal Nath, even my friend Vasant Sathe, in the victims' testimonies. I was told these Congressmen went to Rakab Ganj and other gurdwaras and incited the murderous mobs. I have spoken to Sathe about this, I needed to know. He claims he is innocent. There are other Congress people who I don't doubt had a role in the killings. They all roam free and contest elections.

But there were also people from whom I had never expected support but they came to see me during those days. Arun Shourie, Malgaonkar. I remember that. And the Swedish diplomat—we didn't even know him. He had no reason to do all that he did for us.

When I surrendered the Padma Bhushan in protest of the '84 riots, among the people who condemned me was Vinod Mehta then the editor of the *Observer*. He wrote that when it came to choosing between being an Indian and being a Sikh, I had chosen to be a Sikh. I had never believed that I had to be one or the other. I was both an Indian and a Sikh and proud of being so. I might well have asked Mehta 'Are you a Hindu or an Indian?' Hindus didn't have to prove their nationality; only Muslims, Christians and Sikhs are required to give evidence of their patriotism.

ON THE 1984 RIOTS

As for the Nanavati Report, it was utter rubbish. I have all 349 pages of the inquiry report as well as the Action Taken Report presented by Prime Minister Manmohan Singh's government in Parliament on 8 August 2005. It is largely based on what transpired in the various police stations in different zones and a long list of names which mean nothing to me. There are broad hints of the involvement of Congress leaders like H.K.L. Bhagat, Jadgish Tytler, Dharam Das Shastri and Sajjan Kumar. Nanavati gives them the benefit of the doubt and suggests yet another inquiry commission to look into the charges against them. Yet another commission? For God's sake, is he serious? What sort of fools does he take us for?

THE SIKHS

For a fairly small minority, the Sikhs are disproportionately successful and visible in Indian society. I think it is the Punjabi spirit of *chardi kala*—never say die. The legendary jovialness of the Sikhs is another reason. You could say that the greater visibility may also be because Sikhs are gregarious and great braggers and boasters!

Am I a Sikh first? No. I'm an agnostic. A free-thinking sybarite! Unlike religious people, I like the good life. But, since I was born a Sikh, I have a sense of belonging to the community. Mostly it is petty things like counting how many Sikhs there are in positions of power. In politics and the top bureaucracy,

THE SIKHS   117

in the armed forces, in sports. When Harbhajan [Singh] does well and wins matches for India, I say 'Shabaash'. I feel chuffed. It is very childish!

When my son Rahul cut his hair and became a Mona, my wife and I were both upset—she more than me, and she said she never wanted to see his face again! I was upset because it seemed to me like a rejection of his community. But then I realized I was overreacting. He had a right to live his life on his terms. What is important to me may not be as important to him, and he may have his own commitment to his history and culture.

I'm concerned about any injustice done to the community, or when it does harm to itself. Then I feel I must speak up. Blue Star, for instance. It was a grave mistake and it hurt every Sikh. The militants had to be flushed out, but storming the Golden Temple was not the way to do it. I returned my Padma Bhushan to the government of India as protest. I felt that was the strongest statement I could make.

Before that, I had been writing against the

violence of the Khalistanis because that is not Sikhism to me. I was called a traitor. I remember landing at Oslo airport once and being greeted with placards that said 'Traitor, go back'! But I continued speaking against the killings and extortion because that kind of terrorism had nothing to do with Sikh identity and pride. It was only after I had returned the Padma Bhushan that the strong feelings against me among hard-line Sikhs abated.

The whole separatist movement was a mistake, and it went horribly wrong. It was suicidal of Sikhs to demand Khalistan. It would have been a small state, relying mainly on agriculture, with Pakistan on one side and India on the other, and not viable at all. It was delusional to talk of a modern version of a Sikh empire. Even that existed only during the lifetime of Maharaja Ranjit Singh. After him, everyone killed each other for the throne and the British took over easily.

During the Khalistan movement, Bhindranwale earned us the hatred of the Hindus. His goons would stop buses on

THE SIKHS

Punjab's highways, line up all the Hindus and gun them down. They would kill or beat up journalists who did not toe their line. No leader stood up to them. Few journalists could afford to, especially in Punjab. Naturally, my criticism wasn't going to be tolerated. The Khalistanis put me on their hit list. For years a poor armed policeman sat outside my house and had to accompany me wherever I went. It was a nuisance.

Those days of massive disaffection, and the Hindu–Sikh divide are now over. The only threat that I can see to Sikhism is that it may lapse into Hinduism. There's a large number of Monas already, especially among the young; they become Hindus who believe in the Sikh gurus. As for the culture, it appears to be in a healthy state. The Punjab government has made Gurmukhi mandatory, so at least the future of our language is okay.

The roots of Sikhism lie in the Bhakti tradition in Hinduism. Guru Nanak picked its most important features: belief in one God who is indefinable, unborn, immortal, omniscient, all-pervasive and the epitome of truth; belief in the guru as the guide in spiritual matters; unity of mankind without caste distinction; rejection of idol worship and meaningless ritual; sanctity of the sangat (congregation) which is expected to break bread together at the langar; the gentle way of approaching God through domestic obligations; singing kirtan (hymns); emphasis on work as a moral obligation. There's little doubt that Nanak felt he had a new message, and that it needed to be conveyed after him. So he started the practice of nominating a successor.

The Sikh community underwent a radical change with Guru Arjan's martyrdom in 1606. And though its creed remained wedded to the Adi Granth, it was ready to defend itself by the use of arms. Guru Arjan's son raised a cavalry of horsemen and build the Akal Takht facing

THE SIKHS

the Harmandir as the seat of temporal power and came to be designated Miri Piri da Malik, the Lord of Temporal and Spiritual Power. The final transition, however, came after Aurangzeb had Tegh Bahadur executed in 1675. It was then that his son Guru Gobind's concept of God underwent a martial metamorphosis. He succeeded in creating a breed of warriors with a do-or-die spirit. When the Sikhs became rulers of the Punjab, Maharaja Ranjit Singh realized the value of having troops of Nihangs whom he threw into battle against the Ghazis.

The determination to never give in or give up is deeply rooted in the Sikh psyche; even in adversity they are expected to remain in buoyant spirits—chardi kala. It is their belief that destiny is in their hands.

A Sikh revival coincided with the Green Revolution and the man who started it was Giani Zail Singh. He wanted to get the better of the Akalis who monopolized the propagation of Sikhism, and as chief minister of Punjab for five years, he ensured that the government had a Sikh orientation. It was Zail Singh, more than anybody else, who presented and promoted the rustic preacher Jarnail Singh Bhindranwale, the man who had brought back into the Khalsa fold thousands of young Sikh boys who had strayed from the path of orthodox Sikhism. He encouraged them to become shastradhari, bearer of arms, added revolvers and rifles to the kirpan and replaced horses with motorcycles. His uncouth village vocabulary was full of disparaging references to Hindus. Bhindranwale discovered that the easiest way to prevent the absorption of the Khalsa into Hinduism was by creating a gulf between Sikhs and Hindus. And for a while he succeeded in splitting the two communities.

It was this period that stands out the most in modern Sikh history. From Bhindranwale's reign to Operation Blue Star, the assassination of Mrs Indira Gandhi and subsequent massacre of the Sikhs, and the ultimate isolation of the Sikh community when they were marginalized and made to feel they did not belong. But the

THE SIKHS 123

tides turned. It happened slowly but it did happen. The Sikhs gradually recovered. For the first time in the history of India there is a Sikh Prime Minister, there was a Sikh as chief of the army [General J.J. Singh, now retired], a Sikh election commissioner [M.S. Gill], and a Sikh is heading the Planning Commission of India [Montek Singh Ahluwalia]. The prophecy 'Raj karega Khalsa' (the Khalsa shall rule) has come true, and the Khalsa is ruling today also through the ballpoint pen!

ON COMMUNALISM

The nineties were dark times for India. Fascism well and truly crossed our threshold and dug its heels in our courtyard. We let the fanatics get away with every step they took without raising a howl of protest. They burnt books they did not like; they beat up journalists who wrote against them; they openly butchered people for believing in a different God.

The carnage in Gujarat, the Mahatma's home state, in early 2002, and the subsequent landslide victory for Narendra Modi, spelt disaster for our country. The fascist agenda of Hindu fanatics is unlike anything India has experienced in its modern history. The saffron

ON COMMUNALISM

tide was rising and I was very afraid that it would destroy the nation. For the first time, I was seriously concerned for the country's future. Modi is a murderer. And Advani and he have a symbiotic relationship—they help each other. Modi helps Advani win elections from Gandhinagar and Advani in turn exonerates him from the charges of the 2002 Gujarat riots.

I feel strongly about the communal cries of certain political parties—especially the parties that believe in Hindutva.

Soon after the Babri masjid was destroyed I'd asked the BJP's K.R. Malkani 'How many more mosques will you destroy? What about the repercussions? Hasn't the atmosphere been fouled forever?'

There's been one incident after another ever since. The killing of Christians in Kandhamal, Muslims in Gujarat, the Bangalore pub incident, the venom in Varun Gandhi's speech. If you spare such intolerant people full of hatred you breed many more. But we never seem to punish the culprits who are fouling the atmosphere.

Has anyone been punished for the Gujarat pogrom, for the Mumbai riots? In fact, the recommendations based on the findings of the Srikrishna Commission report have not been implemented till date.

Advani's rath yatra from Somnath to Ayodhya leading to the destruction of the Babri Masjid on December 6, 1992 was the one event that pitchforked him to the centrestage and reshaped India's politics. Advani, more than anyone else, sensed that Islamophobia was deeply ingrained in the minds of millions of Hindus and it needed only a spark to set it ablaze. He claims that breaking the mosque was not on his agenda; that he actually sent Murli Manohar Joshi and Uma Bharati to plead with those who went on the rampage to desist. If that is so, why were the two seen embracing each other and rejoicing when the nefarious task was completed? We don't have to wait for the

ON COMMUNALISM 127

verdict of the Liberhan Commission to tell us what happened; we saw it with our own eyes.

At an event at the IIC I even told Advani to his face, in front of an audience, 'You have sowed the seeds of communal disharmony in the country and we are paying the price for it.'

In his memoir he recorded the jubilation that followed at the site along with his triumphal return to Delhi. The repercussions were worldwide. Enraged Muslims targeted Hindu and Sikh temples—from Bangladesh to the UK. And in India, relations between Hindus and Muslims have never been the same. There were communal confrontations in different parts of the country: the serial blasts in Mumbai, the attack on the Sabarmati Express in Godhra and the massacre of innocent Muslims in Gujarat can all be traced back to the fall of the Babri Masjid.

However, the BJP got what it wanted. It reaped a rich electoral harvest, winning many of the elections that followed, and eventually installed Atal Behari Vajpayee as prime minister and L.K. Advani as his deputy. Advani is now their candidate for the top job and he asserts that he will not allow the Babri Masjid to be rebuilt.

The one time Advani faltered in his steps was when he visited Karachi in 2005. He had praised the speech Jinnah had made at the Pakistan Constituent Assembly on August 11, 1947, calling it 'a classic exposition of a secular state'. It might well have been so, but Jinnah's speech was delivered at a time when millions of Hindus and Sikhs were being driven out of Pakistan or being slaughtered and an equal number of Muslims driven out of India. It was the bloodiest exchange in which over a million died and over 10 million were uprooted. Advani's eulogy must have pleased Pakistanis. It was badly received in India, particularly by his colleagues in the RSS and BJP.

The RSS and BJP have realized after the 2009 elections that they are on the wrong track. I think that the downfall of the BJP has begun. They won't be able to gather the mass support that they want. At least Manmohan Singh apologized in Parliament for what was done to the Sikhs in 1984. The BJP should apologize for the Babri Masjid demolition and for the Muslim massacre in the 2002 Gujarat riots.

All along, the one thing that has dictated the parties that preach Hindutva—their one motivating factor—has been Islamophobia. Their agenda has been anti-Muslim and they have been untied in that. In fact today, when Mohan Bhagwat says that the RSS is open to other communities and has Muslim and Christian members as well it has to be taken with a pinch of salt. I feel that today the general public has rejected their policy of violence and hatred. At least, that's what I hope.

People all over the world are feeling more insecure today than ever before. And they are seeking refuge in their religion.

I've always wanted to bridge the gap between Sikhs and Muslims. When I was awarded the Rockefeller Fellowship in the late fifties, I decided to write the two volumes on the history of the Sikhs under the auspices of the Aligarh Muslim University. Atal Behari Vajpayee had raised this issue in parliament, saying he saw a sinister move in it.

In 1999, when the Christian missionary Graham Staines was brutally burned to death while he slept in his car with his two little sons, I wrote against the attacks. And I wrote strongly against the violent attacks against Christians in Kandhamal two years ago.

A great majority of English-speaking Indians have at some stage of their lives been to missionary schools or colleges or a hospital managed by missionaries, and nobody has ever tried to convert these Indians there. I think we have no gratitude for those who have served us selflessly. In fact, when Arun Shourie wrote about conversions, hitting out at Christians, I pointed out to him that he owed his own education to the Christian missionaries. Then when he wrote against Islam and fatwas I cornered him again. I even invited him home to dine with some of my Muslim friends to show him that he's wrong about what he says about the Muslim community. He's even written against Ambedkar. But the situation is grave. It is really upsetting. Earlier, the CIA was blamed for all our problems. Once when some students clashed with the police over cinema tickets, Giani Zail Singh said the CIA had a hand in it. Now it is the ISI. And Pakistan, mind you, is using the same strategy. There, they blame RAW for all their problems.

It's not just a Hindu-Muslim problem. Nor a Hindu-Christian one. We have become intolerant. We have no compassion or understanding for those who are different from us.

I think most Indians don't realize the

magnitude of the communal problem in our country—in spite of the signs being writ large in recent years. The intolerance that people have shown—and the politicians have fanned these flames—is disgraceful. The way Husain's paintings were burnt, or the shooting of a film stopped, or the way changes were introduced in history books and school texts, the hate propaganda against the Christians and Muslims—false theories that the Christian population is going up because of conversions when in fact the reality is that the Christian population in India has actually gone down. And the Sangh capitalizing on old prejudices about Muslims—that they are multiplying at an alarming rate when the census figures clearly show that the rate of growth of the Hindu population has always been higher ... Since Independence, in almost every communal riot, the Muslim loss of life and property has been almost ten times that of the Hindus. It's a sad day for the country if Muslims have to survive like the Hindus and Christian minorities do in Pakistan.

ON COMMUNALISM 133

This communal violence, these prejudices, is what worries me the most about this country. I'm not optimistic but one should fight, one should make every single effort to save the country and openly challenge and take on the men who are creating trouble and destroying the country. We have to battle with them at any cost, give it back to them, abuse for abuse. If we love our country we have to save it from these communal forces. Even though the liberal class is shrinking I do hope that the present generation totally rejects communal and fascist polices.

ON POLITICS TODAY

We seem to be on the right course. The Sonia and Manmohan combination is working out well. The 2009 elections were decisive—it was to be either the right wing or the secular parties. And the greatest relief is that the fundoos have been put down.

One thing that bothers me though is that even though we call ourselves a secular democracy the State involves itself in religious matters. I'm referring to the way hectares of forest land were given to the Amarnath Shrine Board, creating total chaos and anarchy in the state of J&K. It's okay to look after the security and comfort of pilgrims but to give away public

ON POLITICS TODAY

property or money to religious bodies is not done in a secular state. The same can be said about the way the Government of India sends official delegations of Muslims to Haj. Why should the government send delegations and provide subsidies for the pilgrims? Why this government patronage? There is no justification for doing this in a secular democracy.

I am totally disillusioned with the Left. They seem fixated on their anti-American position. Today we are the closest allies of America, but the way the Left react to any kind of talks with the US, it's not good for our country. It was especially disturbing and upsetting, the manner in which the Communists withdrew support to the Manmohan Singh government last year. They just pulled out and joined hands with certain factions of the communal parties of this country—and this when the Left are sworn enemies of the right wing.

They opposed the nuclear deal which will be of immense benefit to us. They continue to take a pro-Chinese stand even though we have been victims of Chinese aggression for a long time. It's good that the country gave their verdict against the Left in the last general elections—I hold Prakash Karat chiefly responsible for their defeat.

My disillusionment with the Left began years ago, when Stalin made his pact with Hitler. It had shocked me because in my student days I was a strong supporter of the Left and canvassed for the candidates. (In the Punjab there were separate electorates.) I'd not just voted for the Communists but had even housed Daniel Latifi and two of his Communist friends who were on the run in my home in Lahore. One was Sripad Dange and the other Ajoy Ghosh.

It is impossible to predict the future in this country. A single event can transform things, usually for the worse—an assassination, a war, a bad election. But as things are today, and if nothing catastrophic happens, India seems to be in good hands. The country is safe with this trio [Manmohan Singh, Sonia Gandhi and Rahul Gandhi].

ON PAKISTAN

I'm often criticized for being pro-Pakistan. But wanting good relations with Pakistan is being pro-India.

Pakistan is the country of my roots, the land of my birth. I will always have deep affection for that country. Each time I visited my village Hadali, where I was born and spent my formative years, and where our ancestral home still lies, I was overcome with emotion. After I left the village as a child and had shifted to Delhi with my grandmother, I'd visited Hadali three times—twice before Partition and once many years after. And each time I stood feeling overwhelmed, choked. Each time I was flooded with memories of my grandmother—how she'd take me with her when she visited various families in the neighbourhood; to the dharamsala, to the granthi, how she cooked, cleaned the place . . . her voice.

I was always warmly received by the villagers. Three Muslim families who'd shifted from Rohtak were living in our ancestral house and they were so happy to meet me. A few years ago Minoo Bhandara got photographs of our home in the village. They have a board outside the main entrance the house inscribed: 'In this haveli was born Khushwant Singh, eminent novelist, historian and promoter of Indo-Pakistan friendship'.

I've had the opportunity of meeting both Bhutto and his successor Zia. I first met Bhutto in Manzur Qadir's house in Lahore. Manzur was then Ayub Khan's foreign minister. He was receiving visitors while I was alone in his study

ON PAKISTAN 139

when a handsome, dapperly dressed young man walked in. Manzur came in and said, 'I see you have introduced yourselves.' When I said we had not, Manzur told me that Zulfikar was the youngest minister in the cabinet. I left the room and let them talk in private. Manzur was later dropped from the cabinet because Bhutto denounced him as a free thinker and not a good Muslim. He resumed legal practice and retired as chief justice of the Punjab High Court.

Bhutto invited me to Pakistan when he was in power. Our first meeting was in Karachi. Even though he pandered to the Muslim clergy and their archaic laws because he wanted their support—and had even banned the consumption of liquor—we had drinks on his lawn. Two days later, I spent another evening with him in Islamabad and had a second round of drinks. He asked me to convey a message to Indira Gandhi: he was anxious to be on friendly terms with India. When I returned to Delhi I sought an appointment with Mrs Gandhi and conveyed Bhutto's message of goodwill to her. She gave her opinion in one sentence: 'He is a damned liar.'

I was in Islamabad for an interview with General Zia-ul-Haq when Bhutto was hanged, staying in a posh hotel largely occupied by foreign journalists. My appointment with the President was a ruse to mislead the foreign media—after all, he would never grant an interview to an Indian after hanging Bhutto, would he! The next morning, when I looked out of my window and saw the hotel surrounded by tanks and armoured cars I rang up our ambassador Shankar Bajpai and told him. 'I'll get back to you in a few minutes,' he said. He rang back to say, 'They have done the deed.' My appointment with Zia was postponed by a week. A week later, when I was back in Islamabad, General Zia received me with great courtesy. My first question was, 'General sahib, was it necessary to hang Bhutto? Could you not have pardoned him?' He replied: 'He was convicted of murder, for which the punishment is death. Forgiveness is not in man's hands, it can only be given by Allah.'

Because Pakistan and India have wasted so much of our energies on the next conflict, we are both the architects of each other's economic ruin. During Musharraf's regime, which coincided with Vajpayee's time, I'd made no secret of the fact that our relations with Pakistan couldn't have been better. There was an increase in Indo-Pak cross-border traffic. That was good for relations between the two neighbours. We still occasionally hear of politicians, singers, poets, and film personalities who come and go, but rarely do we hear of artists exhibiting their works outside their countries. M.F. Husain and the late F.N. Souza received wide acclaim in Pakistan. We need more of our painters and artists visiting Pakistan and it is high time that Indians got to see what Pakistani artists are up to. There should be more exhibitions of each other's works.

Today I haven't the foggiest idea what's happening in Pakistan. Even the Pakistanis don't know. And now they have chosen a man who is notoriously corrupt. Zardari had a suspended jail term in Switzerland for indulging in shady deals. He is known as 'Mister Ten Per Cent' for brokering deals with the government when his wife Benazir was in power. In spite of two terms of office as head of state, Benazir had failed to introduce any legislation to improve the living conditions of the people of Pakistan. Instead she had acquired vast real estate in England, France, the US and Switzerland.

The signs aren't very hopeful, even though in the last elections Muslim fundoos were routed in the areas they controlled and the liberals won. But where I feel uneasy is that they picked a nondescript politician as prime minister who poses no threat to Zardari and the kingmaker is Zardari who inspires no confidence in anyone.

I worry at times when I think about what's going on in the subcontinent, in our neighbouring countries. There is so much violence, senseless killings and assassinations. And what's troubling is the air of aggression and suspicion which has existed for years. We blame ISI for all our problems and Pakistan blames RAW for theirs. What will this achieve? Where will this take us? And just as we have our set of Hindu fundamentalists here, they have theirs—Muslim fundoos—responsible for the senseless massacres and blasts.

I continue to receive many visitors from Pakistan. They come to meet me when they're in Delhi. It used to be a tradition of sorts—the newly appointed High Commissioner of Pakistan to India would first call on me. And though I see no one without a prior appointment, with those who come from Pakistan I make an exception.

Today, all my Pakistani friends from my Lahore days are gone, and though I still get invitations to travel to Pakistan I can't take the journey.

TERROR AND 26/11

My son who lives Colaba rang up at 9.30 p.m. on November 26 to tell us about the bomb blasts and assure us that he was safe. I switched on my TV. I saw flames billowing out of windows of the Taj hotel and its dome enveloped in smoke. I had lived close by for many years and was a daily visitor to its health club. I saw the Oberoi, where I had stayed a few times, surrounded by Indian commandos and guests looking out of windows. I saw the devastation caused to the Jewish enclave, Victoria Terminus, Cama Hospital and the airport. I was numb with disbelief. I had spent many happy years in the city. My first reaction was of impotent rage: 'Hang the bloody bastards on Marine Drive and let the world see how we deal with murderers of innocent people!'

I cooled down and watched scenes repeated over and over again. They had no leads on the perpetrators. All I could gather was that they knew their way about Mumbai very well, had been fully trained and equipped with the most lethal weapons. They must have also known there was little chance of their ever getting back to their homes. By the time I switched off the TV, the death toll was over 90, including two police officers investigating the Malegaon blast case. They also reported that one of the culprits had been shot dead. I hoped and prayed that he didn't turn out to be a Muslim.

Alas. He was. So was the rest of the gang. All Pakistanis. From the meticulous way the operation was carried out, it was evident that they had been rehearsing it in minute detail for many weeks, if not months, on Pakistani soil. Pakistan's rulers had a great deal to explain to the whole world. Many of the victims include foreign nationals.

The Mumbai attacks dealt a heavy blow to those who have been trying to build bridges between the people of India and Pakistan. The process must continue. At the same time we must do our very best to put down those who are likely to exploit the murderous assault in Mumbai to spread Islamophobia. Many Indian Muslims were killed; all of them condemn it, as do other Indians—Hindus, Christians, Sikhs, Buddhists and Parsis alike. If we do not stand united in our reactions to what had happened in Mumbai, the murderers will have achieved what they wanted to achieve. We must not allow this to happen. We are one nation. We must give them one answer: to hell with you! You will never succeed in dividing us.

The star performer in the tragedy was Mohammad Ajmal Amir aptly surnamed Kasab, the butcher. He and nine of his co-murderers killed over 171 Indian men and women, Hindus, Sikhs, Muslims, Christians, as well as half a dozen foreigners within a few hours. They destroyed property worth thousands of crores and virtually brought tourist traffic down to a standstill, depriving many more thousands of their daily livelihood.

Kasab admitted to his crime in open court and pleaded with the judge that he punish him for what he did. He named several Pakistanis and an Indian, Abu Jundal, as co-conspirators. There can be no doubt that his confession was voluntary and no kind of pressure was put on him to do so. He must know that the only punishment for a crime of this magnitude is to be hanged by the neck till you are dead. The judge very wisely delayed pronouncing the sentence to give Kasab a chance to retract his confession.

It was obvious right from the start that there had to be more than one Indian involved in the elaborate and meticulously carried out carnage. It was up to the governments of Pakistan and India to prove that when they said they would co-operate in stamping out terrorism they meant business.

It is clear now that we should not expect an honest response from Pakistan's leaders. The north-western half of Pakistan is firmly in the grip of backward-looking mullah-mentors of jihadi gangsters. Pakistan's army, prodded by the Americans, wages a half-hearted war on them because they are fellow-Pakistanis and fellow-Muslims. They would rather engage in battles against Americans and Indians, neither of whom are Muslims. Nobody is quite sure of the role being played by its intelligence services which is often accused of patronizing jihadis. We are even less sure of who is in control of Pakistan's nuclear arsenal and who has the power to press the fatal button. The scene is so utterly confusing that it is impossible to think clearly besides concluding that if there is another incident like the Mumbai blasts, both our countries have had it.

On 3 May, Ajmal Amir Kasab, charged with the deaths of 166 Indians and foreigners, was pronounced guilty of all eighty-six charges, by a special court in Mumbai. While delivering the judgement, he was found guilty for murder and waging war against the nation. The two Indians who were named as co-accused in the case were acquitted because the evidence against them was weak. Three days later a trial court gave him the death sentence on four counts and life on five.

Kasab initially put the noose around his own neck and no tears shall be shed for him. And even though I'm against the death penalty—it's inhuman; it should be abolished—when it comes to ghastly crimes like this, I feel the culprits ought to hang. Just as Indira's and Gandhi's killers did. Our system is such that those jailed, the undertrials, they really suffer. There's a huge backlog of pending cases and most of the people in jail can't afford bail. The whole system has just got worse and all we do is talk. Each time there's a new chief justice there are grand statements about reforms but nothing happens.

ON RELIGION

Religion is playing an increasingly important role in the world today. People are turning to religion because of their insecurities. Minorities feel threatened and look towards religion for protection.

I'm an agnostic. I've never been religious. When I was in my late twenties I used to have long arguments with Manzur Qadir about religion. I'd ask him how a man of reason could believe in angels and rebirth and the influence of Saturn . . . and he didn't have any answers for me.

I've spent all my life reading sacred texts of different religions and found that most of the

ABSOLUTE KHUSHWANT

scriptures have passages of great literary merit. I started reading and studying different scriptures and books on religion in the '60s when I had to teach comparative religion at Princeton University and later at Swarthmore College and the University of Hawaii. That's how I know by heart some of the passages from the Quran, the Gita, the Bible, the Granth Sahib—I have less difficulty with the compilations of Sikh scriptures as they are closer to the Punjabi spoken today. Since I can't read Arabic and Sanskrit I read English translations. Translations rarely catch the music of words and I sense I miss a great deal that those who know the languages of the original enjoy in full measure.

But even though I read and re-read these scriptures I'd much rather read Ghalib, Faiz and Iqbal.

We know very little about each other's faiths and scriptures and this is unfortunate. I think it's important—one should try and read as much as possible from the different scriptures.

Especially in a country like ours, made up of so many different people of different faiths. Also a country where there's so much intolerance, so much rigidness where religion is concerned—what with the Hindu fundoos doing 'shudhi karans' and Musalmaan fundoos going on about 'tablighi jamaat'.

If I had to choose a religion to follow, it would be Jainism. It comes closest to agnosticism and the code of ethics to which, as a rationalist, I subscribe. The word 'jain' is derived from 'jina', one who has conquered himself. In the seventies, when I was editor of *The Illustrated Weekly*, I wrote to the chief ministers of all the states that if they imposed a blanket ban on shikar in their states, in honour of Jain Mahavira, I would give them all the publicity they wanted. Eight chief ministers responded to my appeal and banned killing for sport.

I don't judge any religion by its founders or

154 ABSOLUTE KHUSHWANT

what they stood for or their message, but by how it is being actually practised. How its followers its believers behave. What impresses me about Islam is the very dedication of its followers, and it's amazing how the religion had spread—from Arabs sweeping through Central Asia right up to Spain . . . and they were far ahead of the Europeans in every field, be it the arts, sciences, technology. But look at the plight of Islam now. Now there is a focus on only trivial non-issues—whether the hijab or burkha should be worn . . . The real issues, the important things, seem to have bee forgotten— the need for education and learning, the empowerment of women, as laid down in the Quran, in the Hadith. The two most popular verses of the Quran that appear in Muslim mausoleums, including the Taj Mahal, are Sura Yaseen (which festoons the entrance gate) and Ayat-ul-Kursi, the verse of the throne. Of the two, Ayat-ul-Kursi is the more popular. One of my favourite lines of the Hadith, and one that I firmly believe in and practise in my daily life is *La tasabuddhara, Hoo wallahoo* (Don't waste time, time is God).

We know very little about what the Sufis had to offer. Contrary to some biased historical reports that suggest that millions of Indians converted to Islam because of the Muslim invaders, the reality is that it was the Sufis that held sway. They reached out to the people without making any demands or imposing their views. In fact, they reached out to people from different faiths, cutting across class and caste. This is what drew thousands close to Islam. Sufism also had an impact on the saints of the indigenous Bhakti Movement in northern India—saints like Kabir, Namdev, Tukaram, Guru Nanak and other Sikh gurus. No better evidence is to be found of the phenomenon than the inclusion of their hymns in the Guru Granth Sahib, compiled by the fifth Sikh guru Guru Arjan Dev. Even the foundation stone of the Harmandar Sahib in Amritsar was laid by Sufi saint Mian Mir of the Qadriya silsila.

Guru Nanak equated truth with God: *Sachon orey sabh ko; upar sach achar* (Truth above all; above truth truthful conduct).

As a child I learnt my first prayer from my grandmother. I must have been around four years old and we were still living in Hadali. I was scared of the dark and ghosts. So she taught me this prayer; they are lines of Guru Arjan:

> *Tati vao na lagai, parbrahm sharanai*
> *Chaugird hamarey Ram kar dukh*
>   *lagey na bhai*

> No ill winds touch those the
>   great Lord protects
> Lord Rama has drawn his protective
>   circle around you; no sorrows can
>   touch you now.

ON RELIGION   157

Giving is very important in Sikhism. In fact, almost every religion lays emphasis on the act of giving as part of religious obligation and it should be practised without any expectations of gratitude. My parents always gave one tenth of their earnings to the family trust.

The tradition of giving one-tenth of one's earnings (*dasvandh*) is as old as Sikhism. Guru Nanak exhorted his followers:

> *Aklee sahib seviae*
> *Aklee paiye maan;*
> *Aklee parh ke bujhai*
> *Aklee keejey daan*

> Use your brains to serve God,
>   and earn respect;
> Use your brains to read, understand,
>   and give in charity.

And again:

> *Ghall khai keihh hutthan deh;*
> *Nanak raah pachhaaney sheh*

> Earn by efforts and with your hands
> Give some of it away,

Nanak, such people have found the true way.

Guru after Guru lauded the need to give a part of one's earnings to the needy till it becomes a motto: *Kirat karo, naam japo, vand chhako* (Work, take the name of God, and share your earnings with others). Sikhs have spent and given to charity but there seems to be a pattern: Building new gurdwaras is the first priority; schools and hospitals are the second and third. The order needs be reversed. The good thing is that a village gurdwara is not only a place of worship. It is also a community centre and a place for re-affirming bonds of faith.

Sikhs are the richest minority community in the country today—there are highly prosperous farmers, leading industrial houses, princely families, the SGPC (Shiromani Gurdwara Parbandhak Committee) has crores—yet it's unfortunate that illiteracy amongst the Sikhs is 30 per cent. There are high levels of crime and violence in the community and the rate of female foeticide is shamefully high. I have tried to reach out and make a difference through my writings.

Hinduism thrives mostly on legends, on past glories. According to Hindus they are 'peace loving' people but let them ask the Muslims and the Christians of this country how peace loving they actually are. One can't forget that it was Hindus who killed Christians in Kandhamal and it was Hindus who butchered Muslims in Gujarat. They should spend time reading and understanding what their scriptures say. Like this beautiful, powerful line from the Gita, for instance: *Karmanye vadhikar astey ma phaleshu kadachana* (It is in your powers to act but not desire the fruits of your action).

Some of the most beautiful lines of verse are from the Bible:

In the beginning was the Word, and the Word
was with God, and the Word was God.
The same was in the beginning with God.
All things were made by him; and without him
was not any thing made that was made.
In him was life; and the life was the light of
men. And the light shineth in darkness;
and the darkness comprehended it not.

St John, I: 1–5

Though I speak with the tongues of men and
of angels, and have not love, I am become
as sounding brass, or a tinkling cymbal.
And though I have the gift of prophecy, and
understand all mysteries, and all
knowledge; and though I have all faith, so
that I could remove mountains, and have
not love, I am nothing.
And though I bestow all my goods to feed the
poor, and though I give my body to
be burned, and have not love, it profiteth
me nothing.

I Corinthians, 13: 1–3

ON RELIGION

And ye shall know the truth, and the truth shall make you free.

St John, 8: 32

The Bible, translated from Hebrew and Greek, has been polished with every generation, by a succession of scholars. Both the Old Testament and the New Testament have passages of linguistic excellence which have become an integral part of European languages spoken today. Among the many that most Christians know by heart is the Sermon on the Mount, found in the Gospel of St Matthew, usually known as the Beatitudes or Blessings. 'Blessed are the poor in spirit, for theirs is the kingdom of heaven. Blessed are they that mourn, for they shall be comforted. Blessed are the meek, for they shall inherit the earth. Blessed are they who thirst after righteousness, for they shall be filled. Blessed are the merciful, for they shall obtain mercy. Blessed are the pure in heart, for they shall see God. Blessed are they who are persecuted for righteousness' sake, for theirs is the kingdom of heaven. Blessed are you, when men shall revile you, and persecute you, and say all manners of evil against you falsely, for my sake.'

Note the utterly simple language shorn of literary conceits. The strength of the sermon—and of most sacred verse or holy text—lies in its simplicity and directness. The message goes straight into the readers' hearts and stays there forever. The word 'blessed' in this context, does not mean one who is blessed with good luck, but one who is in need of solace. One should keep in mind that the message of the sermon is different from that of the Ten Commandments which spell out a code of conduct on what we should or should not do—don't lie, don't steal, don't usurp another's property, don't commit adultery and so on. The sermon, on the other hand, is an assurance that those who suffer will, by God's grace, be comforted.

ON RELIGION

I have always believed in learning from other faiths and have taken great pleasure in visiting places of worship: temples, mosques, churches, both historic and modern. One of the most spectacular and arresting sights I've ever been witness to is at Haridwar. For hours I have sat on the banks of the river and watched the diyas and boats and flowers and the aarti taking place. It is truly unforgettable. The other place that is special is the Golden Temple. It has the most calming, serene atmosphere you can ever imagine. The moment you enter the premises you feel it.

ON URDU

Maangey Allah se bas itni dua hai Rashid
Main jo Urdu mein vaseeyat likhoon
    beta parh le

All Rashid asks of Allah is just one
    small gift
If I write my will in Urdu, may my son be
    able to read it.

When I was studying in Delhi's Modern School
I was the only student in my class who had
opted for Urdu. The rest had taken Hindi. So,
being his only student, I got close to the Urdu
teacher Maulana Shafiuddin Nayyar. He was
an excellent man and that certainly made a

difference. He wrote poetry and encouraged my interest in Urdu verse. Years later, in Lahore, it was Manzur Qadir who revived my interest in Urdu and Urdu poetry. Once, on a sea voyage back from England, he made me translate Iqbal right till he got off at Karachi. My interest in the language was rekindled when I was in Bombay. It was at the insistence of the Zakarias that I'd translated Iqbal's 'Shikwa' and 'Jawab-e-Shikwa'. I often went to Ali Sardar Jafri for help if I was stuck. I dedicated my collection *Celebrating the Best of Urdu Poetry* to Fatma and Rafiq Zakaria.

Today, Urdu is dying a slow death in the land where it was born and where it flourished. Hardly anyone opts for Urdu as a subject in schools and colleges. Apart from Kashmir, where Urdu is taught from the primary to the post-graduate levels, it is the second or third language in the rest of the country. Over time

166   ABSOLUTE KHUSHWANT

it has come to be known as the language of the Muslims, which is far from the truth. It was always meant to be the language of the masses—branding it as the language of the Muslims is communal propaganda. And this is destroying the language further. Even Muslim families these days prefer their children to learn Hindi or the language of the region in which they live. Knowledge of Urdu cannot ensure getting jobs either in the government or in private business houses, while knowing English, Hindi or a regional language does.

The language evolved over the years, and was influenced by several languages: Turkish, Arabic and Persian (as spoken by the soldiers in the invading armies) together with local languages like Hindi, Sanskrit, Braj—languages spoken by the general population and also by the soldiers and staff with the Mughal rulers. Urdu was a mixture of all these, a connecting language. The very word 'Urdu' means 'camp'. Initially, the well-known poets of the Mughal era had preferred to stick to Persian and had little to do with this language of the masses. They soon realized that in order to reach the masses and have any kind of influence it would have to be Urdu.

Urdu poetry is filled with imagery from Arabic and Persian art and literature. The most popular are the nightingale or bulbul's lament for the unresponsive rose; moths flocking to the candle flame only to incinerate themselves; Majnu's never-ending quest for his beloved Laila, and Farhaad hacking rock-cliffs to get to his Shirin. Almost all Urdu verse is overwhelmingly romantic, and there's a morbid obsession with the passage of time—the decline of youth, old age and, ultimately, death. A mood of despair runs through much of Urdu poetry. But there is also plenty of wit and humour. Later poets used Urdu poetry as a means of social reform, to denounce bigotry and religious hatred.

It seems surprising that while most Urdu poets were and are Muslims, to whom wine is haraam, forbidden, they wrote more on the joys of drinking than on any other subject.

Some, like Ghalib, Sahir and Faiz were even heavy drinkers. Urdu poetry is full of references to the *maikhana*, tavern, and the *saqi*, wine server. However, there is no historical evidence of maikhanas in any city—there were wine shops where liquor could be bought and consumed alone, in exclusively male gatherings or in salons of courtesans. A lot of Urdu poetry is addressed to courtesans. A lot of it is also addressed to rosy-cheeked, round-bottomed boys, who on occasion were the wine servers.

Saqi gayi bahaar dil mein rahi havas
Tu minnaton se jam de aur main
        kahoon ki 'bas!'

O saqi, gone is the spring of youth
Remains but one regret in this
        heart of mine:
Had you but pressed the goblet
        to my hand
Had I but said, 'Enough!'

Zauq jo madarsey ke bigdey huey hain mullah
Unko maikhaney mein le aao sanvar jaengey

The mullahs who've been ruined by the madrassas, O Zauq
Bring them to the tavern, they'll be all right again.

It's only in Bollywood that Urdu is alive today. And that's because of ghazals. Several film-makers still resort to them—not to further the cause of the language—to add to their films' charm. People also use Urdu verse and shairs to impress—they insert them in their speeches, in their debate sessions in Parliament. It's all very well to use a smattering of Urdu verse but what's really crucial is that if we continue to neglect the language this way—to take it off the school and college curriculum—it will soon be dead.

These lines of Khurshid Afsar Bisrani describe its plight:

> *Ab Urdu kya hai ek kothey kee tawaif hai*
> *Mazaa har ek leta hai mohabbat*
>   *kam karte hai*

What is Urdu now but a whore
in a whorehouse
Everyone has fun with her, very few
love her.

DESTINY, LUCK, AND FAITH IN HUMBUG

I don't believe in destiny and I'm not superstitious. But I do think there's something to be said for chance or luck and coincidence. I'm lucky, scribbling away ... I sweat, but there's an element of luck: whatever I write gets published.

I find the belief in Feng Shui, Vaastu, numerology and other such practices laughable. But—I don't know what you'd call this—while working on my book of translations of the hymns of Guru Nanak, I was in Tokyo and woke up quite often in the middle of the night to start work. I felt the hand of the Guru on my shoulder. Maybe it was some sort of make-believe, but whatever it was it gave me comfort and I worked on.

Though I have always been completely put off by religious rituals, once during a severe emotional crisis—when I was having trouble in my marriage—I found solace sitting through the entire night in a gurdwara, the Bangla Sahib. It gave me emotional strength.

As a child, and even much later, I had a terrible phobia of ghosts. While growing up, servants told us stories about ghosts and bhoots and I was petrified. When I was very young I had seen two close relatives die in front of me. I saw my grandfather Sujan Singh's death in Mian Channu. He kept gasping and asking for more medicines. Then he opened his mouth wide as if to yawn, gasped and collapsed on his pillow. My grandmother began wailing loudly, chanting the hymn of death. I was horrified

DESTINY, LUCK, AND FAITH . . . 173

and terrified at the sight of my parents, uncles and relations sobbing like children. Servants told me that they had seen my grandfather's spirit fly out of the room like a puff of smoke and disappear in the sky.

Even more gruesome was watching my aunt, my uncle Ujjal Singh's first wife, die. This was also in Mian Channu. She was expecting her second child. I accompanied my mother who was sent to look after her during her confinement. The foetus had died in her womb and her body had turned septic. Every evening when her bed was brought into the courtyard she had hallucinations. It was whispered that she had brought upon evil on herself by plucking a lemon off a tree in the garden after sunset. It was common belief that anyone who did so was possessed by a witch who could only be rid of by exorcism. Prayer books and a *kirpan* were placed under her pillow. Nothing helped. The *daayan* continued to possess her. One afternoon she had terrible convulsions. Her eyes turned till only the whites could be seen. She bit her tongue till blood flowed from her mouth. She died in great agony. Since her own son Narinder was away, I had to light her funeral pyre. I have never understood why children of my age were exposed to such ghastly scenes. Even today I have the fear of ghosts.

There's a legend behind our family's prosperity. Apparently, a peer sahib blessed our family in Hadali. My grandfather had helped out a peer sahib, Shaida Peer and he'd blessed us. It is said that one year when it rained heavily on the Salt Range, flood waters swept down the rocky ridge carrying with it a Muslim man named Shaida Peer who had climbed on to the thatched roof of his hut. By the time he had floated down to Hadali, he had nothing on him except his loincloth. My grandfather Sujan Singh gave him clothes, made a hut for him near the Muslim graveyard and sent him food. Shaida Peer blessed him, saying, 'I will give

DESTINY, LUCK, AND FAITH . . . 175

your two sons the keys of Delhi and Lahore. They will prosper.' And prosper they did—my father as a building contractor in Delhi; his younger brother Ujjal Singh as one of pre-Partition Punjab's biggest landowners. He later became a Member of the Legislative Assembly and, after Independence, finance minister of Punjab and later its Governor. He ended his career as Governor of Tamil Nadu.

We, as a nation, are superstitious, and though I'm not, you will find Islamic emblems, *ayats* and *suraas* all over my house. They are all gifts that I have received over the years. And from Iran I'd got my granddaughter Naina a taveez with the *Ayat-ul-Kursi* inscribed on it—somebody had presented it to me on my visit there. Many Muslims wear the Ayat-ul-Kursi on their amulets. I have the verse inscribed in bidri and silver on my wall. I got a gold medallion from Tehran which my daughter Mala and then her daughter wore as pendants on their necklaces while taking their exams. I'd like to think it brought them luck.

ON DEATH

At ninety-five I do think of death. I think of death very often but I don't lose sleep over it. I think of those gone; keep wondering where they are. Where have they gone? Where will they be? I don't know the answers—where you go, what happens next. To quote Omar Khayyam: Into this Universe, and Why not knowing/Nor Whence, like Water willy-nilly flowing . . .' and 'There was a Door to which I found no Key/There was a Veil through which I could not see/Some little Talk awhile of Me and Thee/There seemed—and then no more of Thee and Me.'

All my contemporaries—whether here or in

ON DEATH

England or in Pakistan—they're all gone. I don't know where I'll be in a year or two. I don't fear death. What I dread is the day I go blind or am incapacitated because of old age— that's what I fear—I'd rather die than live in that condition. I'm a burden enough on my daughter Mala and don't want to be an extra burden on her.

All that I hope for is that when death comes to me it comes swiftly, without much pain, like fading away in sound slumber. Till then I'll keep working and living each day as it comes. There's so much left to do. I have to content myself by saying these lines of Iqbal: *Baagh-e- bahisht sey mujhey hukm-e safar diya thha kyon?/ Kaar-e-Jahaan daraaz hai, ab mera intezaar kar* (Why did you order me out of the garden of paradise? I have a lot left to do; now you wait for me). So I often tell Bade Mian, as I refer to him from time to time, that he's got to wait for me as I still have work to complete.

I believe in these lines of Tennyson: Sunset and evening star, And one clear call for me/

And may there be no moaning of the bar, When I put out to sea . . . Twilight and evening bell, And after that the dark!/And may there be no sadness or farewell, When I embark . . .

Death is rarely spoken about in our homes, I wonder why. Especially when each one of us knows that death has to come, has to strike; it's inevitable. This line from Yas Yagana says it best: *Khuda mein shak ho to ho, maut mein nahin koee shak* (You may or may not doubt the existence of God, you can't doubt the certainty of death). And one must prepare oneself to face it.

I once asked the Dalai Lama how one should face death and he had advised meditation.

I'm not scared of death; I do not fear it. Death is inevitable. While I have thought about it a lot, I don't brood about it. I'm prepared for it. As Asadullah Khan Ghalib has so aptly put it: *Rau mein hai raksh-e-umar kahaan dekheeye*

ON DEATH   179

thhamey/Nai haath baag par hai na pa hai rakaab mein (Age travels at a galloping pace; who knows where it will stop/We do not have the reins in our hands nor our feet in the stirrups).

I believe in the Jain philosophy that death ought to be celebrated. Earlier, whenever I was upset or low, I used to go to the cremation grounds. It has a cleansing effect, and it worked like therapy for me. In fact, I'd written my own epitaph years ago: 'Here lies one who spared neither man nor God/Waste not your tears on him, he was a sod/Writing nasty things he regarded as great fun/Thank the Lord he is dead, this son of a gun.'

I had even written my own obit in 1943 when I was still in my twenties. It later appeared in a collection of short stories, titled 'Posthumous'. In the piece I had imagined *The Tribune* announcing news of my death it in its front page with a small photograph. The headline would read: Sardar Khushwant Singh Dead. And then in somewhat smaller print:

We regret to announce the sudden death of Sardar Khushwant Singh at 6 p.m. last evening. He leaves behind a young widow, two infant children and a large number of friends and admirers ... Amongst those who called at the late sardar's residence were the PA to the chief justice, several ministers, and judges of the high court.

I had to cope with death when I lost my wife. Being an agnostic I could not find solace in religious rituals. Being essentially a loner I discouraged friends and relatives from coming to condole with me. I spent the first night alone sitting in my chair in the dark. At times I broke down, but soon recovered my composure. A couple of days later, I resumed my usual routine, working from dawn to dusk. That took my mind off the stark reality of having to live alone in an empty home for the rest of my days. When friends persisted in calling and upsetting my equilibrium I packed myself off to Goa to be by myself.

I used to be keen on a burial because with a burial you give back to the earth what you have taken. Now it will be the electric crematorium. I had requested the management of the Bahai faith if I could be buried. Initially they had agreed but then they came up with all sorts of conditions and rules. I had wanted to be buried in one corner with just a peepal tree next to my grave. After okaying this the management later said that that wouldn't be possible and that my grave would be in the middle of a row and not in a corner. I wasn't okay with that—even though I know that once you are dead it makes no difference. But I was keen to be buried in one corner. They also told me later that they would chant some prayers, which again I couldn't agree with because I don't believe in religion or in religious rituals of any kind.

Though I'm quite fit, I know I don't have much time left. I'm coming to terms with death, preparing myself. I only hope it isn't very painful. And since I have no faith in God, nor in the day of judgement, nor in the theory of reincarnation, I have to come to terms with the complete full stop. I have been criticized for not sparing even the dead, but then death does not sanctify a person, and if I find the person had been corrupt, I write about it even when he's gone.

I don't believe in rebirth or in reincarnation, in the day of judgement or in heaven or hell. I accept the finality of death. We do not know what happens to us after we die but one should help a person go in peace—at peace with himself and with the world.

Above all, when the time comes to go, one should go like a man without any regret or grievance against anyone. Allama Iqbal expressed it beautifully in a couplet in Persian: 'You ask me about the signs of a man of faith? When death comes to him, he has a smile on his lips.'

ON MYSELF

'You have only one life so make the best use of it. Don't waste time, for time is worship and not a minute should be wasted.'

I know I am an ugly man. But physical ugliness has never bothered me. Nor has it inhibited me. I have never been concerned with my outward appearance—my untidy turban and unkempt beard. What lies beneath—the real me—is conflicted by emotions of love and hate, general irritability and occasional equipoise, angry denunciation and tolerance of another's point of view, rigid adherence to self-prescribed regimen and accommodation of others' convenience.

Am I a likeable man? I don't know. I've had very few close friends because I've never set much store by friendship. I get easily bored with people and would rather read a book or listen to music.

The one constant in my life has been my love for dogs and children. They've always given me great happiness. I also enjoy food—I've always liked trying different kinds of cuisines and continue to do so in spite of having to use partial dentures. Mughlai and Punjabi food are too heavy for me and I can no longer handle anything too rich. But about twice or thrice a week I order Italian or Chinese or Thai food from restaurants nearby, and the food's delivered to the house.

Lately, my love for Urdu poetry has grown to such an extent that besides the books that I have to review, which are in English, I read only Urdu poetry. I keep Ghalib on my bedside table and an anthology of Urdu poetry on the table beside me where I sit the entire day.

I've always had a great interest in nature—in

ON MYSELF

flowers and trees and in birds. I enjoy
identifying the different birds that visit the
gardens in both my homes—in Delhi and in
Kasauli. I planted many fruit trees in Kasauli
but the monkeys kept destroying them. Most
of the trees in my garden in Sujan Singh Park
have been planted by me—kadam, kusum, a
bush of gardenia, a couple of jasmines, a raat
ki rani and some avocado trees. I placed a bird
bath at one end of the garden which has been
shared, over the years, by sparrow, crows,
pigeons, mynahs and a dozen stray cats that
have made my home theirs. There was a time
when I'd walk every day in the Lodi Gardens,
which is so close to my house. But now I'm
more or less confined at home so I sit in my
garden and spend my time writing or reading,
doing the crossword or just enjoying the peace
and quiet of being alone.

I think the turning point in my life was
when I decided to quit my job as a diplomat.
It was a big risk, giving up that job and deciding
to make a living by writing.

I think the image of 'dirty old man' and the reputation that I have of womanizing come from the fact that I have always written openly and frankly about sex. Most of the sex in my novels are fantasies—after all, I wasn't much of a lover! But I do love the company of women—especially beautiful women who are lively—and they seem to enjoy mine.

I would like to be remembered as someone who made people smile.

POSTSCRIPT

WAS IT WORTHWHILE?

I have been writing columns for Indian and foreign papers for over sixty years. For the last forty years I have written two columns a week which are reproduced in scores of papers in India, in English and in regional languages. My purpose: to inform, amuse, provoke. It has paid me handsome dividends. I am also somewhat of a missionary preaching secularism and denouncing religious fundamentalism. I was perhaps the only journalist who wrote against Bhindranwale and the demand for Khalistan. He put me on his hit list and assigned the killers of General Vaidya, who had eluded the police, to eliminate me. One of them followed me up to Kasauli but was nabbed by police within two miles of his target. After he was interrogated, I was provided police protection round the clock for over ten years. I was taken to court for libel by Jagjit Singh Chauhan, founder of the Khalistan movement. He was awarded one penny as damages by the London Court and the case against me in Chandigarh died with him. I have reason to believe I had a role in killing the demand for Khalistan which I felt was suicidal for the Sikhs and fatal to India.

My present mission is to warn readers against the dangers posed by Hindu fundamentalists. I used to admire L.K. Advani till he launched his rath yatra from Somnath to Ayodhya and had the Babri Masjid destroyed. Since then I have been his bitterest critic. I will continue to oppose fundoos of all religions till the last. Maybe my efforts will be futile but I will persist no matter what the outcome may be. When asked if what I have been doing will be

POSTSCRIPT 189

worthwhile, in my reply I quote an Urdu couplet:

Kya poochho ho haal merey karobaar ka
Aaeeney bechta hoon andhon ke sheher mein

You ask me about my business, what I
    have in mind
I sell mirrors in the city of the blind.